The Peace I Leave With You

Forty Reflections on the Father, Son, and Spirit for the People of God

For personal study and retreat

by

Bishop Kenneth J. Povish

Edited by Heidi Hess Saxton

Proceeds from this book will go to support vocations for the priesthood.

The Peace I Leave With You
by Bishop Kenneth J. Povish

Printed in the United States of America

ISBN 1-594670-70-6

Scripture references, unless otherwise noted, have been taken from
the Revised Standard Version of the Bible, Catholic Edition. © 1946,
1952, 1971 by the Division of Christian Education of the National
Council of the Churches of Christ in the USA. All rights reserved.

This work is based on the author's collected writings, including but
not limited to his columns in *FAITH* Magazine and *The Catholic
Times.* Selected prayers composed by the editor are indicated by
(hhs). Passages from the *Catechism of the Catholic Church* are indicated by "CCC." All rights reserved.

Cover photo by Christine Jones

Xulon Press
www.XulonPress.com

Xulon Press books are available in bookstores everywhere, and on
the Web at www.XulonPress.com.

Table of Contents

Introduction

S ome time ago, the editors of *Faith* magazine suggested that I write about my experience of cancer, from the time I was diagnosed in 1994 to remission later that year and from its return in 1999 to the present. The people of the diocese have a big role in this story, and I am glad to oblige.

Most of the time, the disease itself has been painless, even when I passed blood in Lent 1994 and lost fourteen pounds in a few weeks in Advent 1999. The suffering was in the cure – radiation therapy and chemotherapy are accompanied by nausea, diarrhea, and perpetual fatigue.

From the beginning there was no questioning, "Why me?" Cancer afflicts people everywhere at any time. So the question is really, "Why not me?" Moreover, as a priest for going on fifty years, when I was stricken I had to be honest and practice what I preached. I can't tell you how many times in parish ministry I counseled or tried to comfort families with words like these: "You say the Lord's Prayer every day. You say, 'Thy will be done on earth as it is in heaven.' Most of the time those words are easy to say, but sometimes you really have to mean it. This is one of those times."

So that has been the addendum I put on all my prayers for healing before saying, "Amen": "Father, Thy will be done." I put that same addendum on your prayers, when I was getting literally bushels of mail telling me you were praying for me at home and also publicly on Sundays at Mass. I prayed every day along these lines: "Father, bless all those who are praying for my recovery. Listen to their petitions, but may your will be done."

Your cards and letters kept my spirits up, and I was especially encouraged by the many cancer survivors who wrote to me. "Hang in there, Bishop," they typically wrote. "I had what you got eight (or ten or twelve) years ago, and I'm still around. Don't give up. We're pulling for you." A positive attitude, the doctors kept telling me, is all-important in fighting cancer; and in the Communion of Saints you all have helped me have it.

It is amazing how a deadly disease raises the intensity level of one's prayer life. I could write a couple pages on that alone, but I will give just two examples from the Liturgy of the Mass. In the altar book there is a prayer for the celebrant to say privately before he takes Holy Communion and another to say quietly while the chalice is being cleansed afterwards. For fifty years I recited these prayers almost without thinking. They mean much more to me now.

Before Communion: "Lord Jesus Christ, with faith in your love and mercy I eat your Body and drink your Blood. Let it not bring me condemnation, but rather health in mind and body." After Communion: "Lord may I receive these gifts in purity of heart. May they bring me healing and strength, now and forever." These two short daily prayers seem ready-made for my condition, and they sustain me daily.

Editor's Note: In a recent interview with Father Charles Irvin, Bishop Povish was characteristically self-deprecating when he compared his own journey to that of his friend Joseph Cardinal Bernardin. "Joe had a touch, a gift that I don't think I have, in that when he had his cancer… he made an apostolate out of it. But one of the things that I pray for is that in this cancer I have now, which is worse than what I had five years ago, that I will give people an example of accepting what God sends and living it in a redemptive way. I'm offering it all up. If this is going to be the end, I want to go out in a way that is a credit to God and something of an inspiration to other people."

It was, and he did. Bishop Povish celebrated his fiftieth year as a priest and his thirtieth year as a bishop in June 2000. Throughout the course of his ministry, Bishop Povish embodied his episcopal motto, "To Accomplish His Work." This work continued right up to the time of his death on September 5, 2003. This book is the fruit of that effort.

Section One

As a Father Loves His Children

ONE

Finding God in the Desert

*No one has ever accomplished much for God
who did not spend time alone with Him in prayer.*

Very Reverend Lloyd P. McDonald, Rector
Theological College, Washington, D.C.

If you live in Michigan, it isn't easy to grasp either the reality or the symbolism of the desert. Surrounded by the world's greatest fresh-water lakes, we live in a Water Wonderland. So when we read the Old Testament accounts of Israel in the desert, or when the Gospel tells us Jesus spent forty days in the desert before beginning His public ministry, the significance of the desert is lost upon us. When spiritual writers or preachers speak of "desert experiences," we are apt not to know what they mean.

It helps if one has seen a desert. As a tourist in Egypt in 1956, I flew over the edges of the Sahara Desert. Its expansive monotony was inspiring. The desert is quiet and mostly lifeless, breathtaking in its own way.

The desert is also hostile. The winds that create sand dunes that appear almost musical can also create sandstorms that are lethal. The desert is waterless. Since the bodies of human creatures are two-thirds water, to get lost in a desert means almost certain death.

The people of Israel first met Yahweh in the desert, and the story of their desert wandering remains the type of human encounters with God. It was also in the desert that Israel was tested, failed, and ultimately found favor with Yahweh. Jesus went into the desert, and passed forty days there in prayer and fasting, alone with His

Father. It was at the end of the forty days that Jesus was tempted by the devil in the desert. The Holy Forty Days of Lent are modeled after Jesus' desert experience.

The forty days of Lent have always been a special time of preparation for the Easter joy to come. However, the disciplines of Lent — prayer, self-denial, and almsgiving – are a proven means of allowing God to act in our lives and to use us for His purposes at any time. Similarly, spiritual reading – whether Scripture, classic spiritual writings, or reflections such as those found in this book – may be read with benefit at any time of year.

Our Lord was often drawn away to a lonely place to spend time with His Father. Of course, not everyone has the luxury of being able to spend forty days in solitary retreat. However, a regular habit of daily prayer and meditation is a necessary part of the spiritual life.

May this little book guide you as you cultivate these important practices in your own life. If you are just getting started, don't worry if it takes a little time for the habit to "take," or wonder if you are doing it "right" or for "long enough." If you miss a day, just begin again. Always remember the promise Jesus gave His disciples before returning to the Father.

"Peace I leave with you; my peace I give to you;
not as the world gives do I give to you.
Let not your hearts be troubled, neither let them be afraid."
John 14:27

TWO

Experiencing God as Father

———⇒●⇐———

*In the sacred books, the Father who is in heaven
comes lovingly to meet his children, and talks with them.*

CCC 102

Each year at the Easter Vigil, as the newly baptized share fully
for the first time in the Eucharist, they join the rest of the faithful in saying or singing the family prayer that our Savior taught us –
the Lord's Prayer or the "Our Father." Many of those who join the
Church come to us already familiar with this prayer. Some recite it
regularly; others have heard believers pray it, either in person or
through the media.

The Church considers the Lord's Prayer a precious family
possession, to be shared with newcomers to the faith. From ancient
times the Lord's Prayer has been the prayer proper to those who in
baptism have received the spirit of adoption. Only the baptized have
the right to call the Creator God "Abba," a title of familiarity that in
the Semitic languages means "Daddy."

Sadly, there are those for whom this joy-filled intimacy is
difficult to grasp. Last week I saw a striking poster. A little boy was
looking with wonder and love on the face of his father. The caption
read: "A child is not likely to find a father in God unless he finds
something of God in his father."

Conservative columnist Cal Thomas once wrote, "Our econ-
omy may be doing well, but we are a sick people. When kids take
up guns and start shooting and killing other kids, it doesn't get any
worse. The leading economic indicators continue to rise; but the

moral, cultural, and social indicators are in a deep depression."

Fathers are not totally responsible for this situation, but they are responsible for a lot of it. With forty percent of the children in this nation growing up without a father in the house, society is in real trouble. Harried working mothers have little time for their children, who are day-cared or left to themselves. No wonder when kids cry out for help, as many do in different ways, the help never comes. If children have no experience of a present, caring, loving, providing father at home, they are not apt to understand what Jesus meant about a present, caring, loving, providing Father in heaven.

Is there a child in your life who needs that kind of tender, loving care from you – if only as a "supplemental parent"? In this way, you too have a hand at bringing about the answer to our prayer:

*"... Thy kingdom come, Thy will be done
on earth as it is in heaven..."*

THREE

Glory in the Storm

———►●◄———

The God of glory thunders, the Lord over the vast waters.
The voice of the Lord is mighty, the voice of the Lord is majestic.
The voice of the Lord breaks in pieces the cedars.
He makes (the mountains of) Lebanon leap like a calf,
and Mount Hermon like a young bull...
The voice of the Lord strikes fiery flames;
the voice of the Lord shakes the desert.
The voice of the Lord twists the oaks and strips the forests bare.
And in his temple, they all cry, "Glory!"

Psalm 29

King David wrote this psalm after watching a terrific thunderstorm come in off the coast of the Mediterranean Sea. He didn't know much about meteorology; seven times the man of faith attributes the crashing thunder directly to God's voice. He pictures the mountains as trembling with fear....

When hurricanes, tornadoes, flash floods, and other catastrophes strike, many people collect insurance for damages caused by what is legally classified as "an act of God." This ancient term comes from English law, and acknowledges that the physical laws that come from "Mother Nature" find their true source in Nature's God.

We, too, can see God both in the storms and their aftermath. The gale winds, lighted skies, and crashing thunder reveal how weak and puny we are in the face of natural forces. A day without electricity shows just how dependent we are on so many things.

Not so with Christ. One of the seven sacred signs of His

divinity revealed by St. John's Gospel was a nature miracle. In John 6:16-24, Jesus astonished and frightened His apostles by walking on water. Jesus calmed them with a majestic statement: "It is I. Do not be afraid." The Greek words used by St. John, *"ego eimi,"* can also be translated simply, "I am." With these words, Jesus communicated to the frightened disciples His divine presence. Even in the storm, they had no need to fear.

The same is true for us today. There is nothing in life – or in death – of which we need to be afraid. Our Heavenly Father will guide us through every storm.

FOUR

Rescued Out of the Depths

—————

Out of the depths I cry to thee, O Lord!
Lord, hear my voice! Let thy ears be attentive
to the voice of my supplications!...
I wait for the Lord, my soul waits, and in his word I hope;
my soul waits for the Lord more than watchmen for the morning.

Psalm 130:1-2, 5-6

In Psalm 130, David pleads for God's forgiveness, "...because with the Lord there is mercy and fullness of redemption." As we turn our thoughts to center on the Passion that brought about our redemption, we think of two of the apostles from the Passion narrative.

Both Peter and Judas illustrate this rescue "from the depths." Both men were sinners – in fact, both committed the same sin. They betrayed Jesus of Nazareth. According to the poet Dante, both of them yielded to the worst of crimes – betraying a dear friend.

Note how differently they ended up. Peter became the chief of apostles and the leader of the new Christian faith. Judas died in disgrace, a shell of a man, a suicide. What made the difference? Peter realized that no one could sink so low that the mercy and power of Christ cannot raise him up – a lesson Judas either did not listen to or did not comprehend.

The Lord Jesus came to earth to reveal to us the heart of the Father. His ministry was characterized by forgiving and healing as much or even more than it was characterized by His teaching. It is by all means significant in the Gospel that Jesus is portrayed as declaring that He healed the body "that you may know that the Son of Man has authority on earth to forgive sins" (Mark 2:10).

A true encounter with Jesus the Christ leads people to an awareness of their sins and their alienation from God; the call to the kingdom means leaving one's past and embracing a new way of living. The wonder of Christianity is that it uncovers the sinful nature of so much conduct, not to plunge us into despair but to offer God's reconciliation and healing.

The Catholic community experiences forgiveness of sins through the sacraments. Baptism forgives all sins and gives us a new birth. Sin is also healed in the Eucharist, "given for you and for all so that sins may be forgiven." In the case of serious sin after baptism, Penance reconciles the sinner again with God and the Christian community according to the Easter promise, "Receive the Holy Spirit. Whose sins you forgive are forgiven them, and whose sins you retain are retained."

Today as we consider our own lives, both the blessings that have come our way and the human failings that have left their mark, let us remember to thank our Father God for the many times He has pulled us "out of the depths."

FIVE

Take My Hand, Lord

For I, the Lord your God, hold your right hand;
It is I who say to you, "Fear not, I will help you."

Isaiah 41:13

Hands are an expressive part of our bodies. Clenched in fists, they signal anger. Pointing a finger, they denote accusation. Thrown up into the air, they indicate helplessness. In team sports, referees and umpires declare judgments with their hands.

The hands of our Lord were expressive, too. Touching people with compassion, they healed. Folded in prayer, they multiplied loaves and fishes. Upraised at the Ascension, they meant blessing.

As we heard in the Holy Gospel proclaimed Thursday, "Then he led them out near Bethany, and with hands upraised, blessed them. As he blessed them, he left them and was taken up to heaven…" (Luke 24:50-51).

This, then, was the last view the disciples had of our Savior in His earthly life – nail-scarred hands raised in blessing over them. No wonder the disciples "returned to Jerusalem filled with joy." No wonder the details were remembered years later when St. Luke penned his gospel.

Ascension Day was the same occasion, the first gospel notes, when Jesus assured His disciples, "I am with you always, until the end of the world" (Matthew 28:20). That is the way we ought to view our Savior today. He is with us, His hands upraised in blessing over us. In dew and sunshine, in temptation and trouble; in sickness and sorrow, in joy and relief; in success and achievement, in danger and even death.

Jesus is not off in some secluded heaven, unaware and unconcerned. He is near, holding loving, living hands upraised in blessing over us. As we try to cope with our bad habits, addictions, personal problems, or discouragement, this assurance gives us hope to face the future. In the words of our Lord: "Seek first [God's] kingship over you, his way of holiness, and all these things will be given you besides. Enough, then, of worrying about tomorrow. Let tomorrow take care of itself. Today has troubles enough of its own" (Matthew 6:33-34).

The following prayer-poem is based on this wisdom:

Lord, for tomorrow and its needs I do not pray.
Keep me, my God, from stain of sin just for today.
Let me both diligently work and duly pray.
Let me be kind in word and deed just for today.
Let me be slow to do my will, prompt to obey.
Help me to mortify my flesh just for today.
Let me no wrong or idle word unthinking say.
Let me be faithful to your grace just for today.
So for tomorrow and its needs I do not pray.
But keep me, guide me, love me, Lord… just for today.

Section Two

Images of Christ in the Gospels

SIX

Ancient Signs of Hope

*"...the New Testament lies hidden in the Old,
and the Old Testament is unveiled in the New."*

St. Augustine [CCC 136]

Ours is a religion of symbols and signs. Ancient pagan religions had them, too, but biblical symbols differ in one essential respect: They point to a Savior.

The Tree of Life. The most familiar "sacred tree" in our day is the Maypole, which forms the center for the sports and dances connected with spring. But the tree has always played an important part in folklore and myth. Trees symbolize the eternal cycle of life and death and rebirth, from spring buds to summer leaves to autumn withering and back to spring again.

All this symbolism of the tree found its fulfillment in Christ. He is foreshadowed in the tree of life that was planted in the midst of Paradise (Gen 3:24). Christ is the "tender twig that is planted on the high mountains of Israel..." according to Ezekiel (17:22-24). This symbol of the tree foretells salvation through the Messiah, and prefigures the risen Christ, true Vine of which we are the branches (John 15:1-8). Because of the Lord's self-giving love, the cross itself is transformed from an instrument of destruction to a symbol of hope. The Good Friday liturgy calls the cross the "tree of mercy, tree of triumph."

The Burning Bush. In Exodus 3:1-15, we read of a fiery encounter between God and Moses, who was tending sheep on Mt. Horeb. The burning bush captured the attention of Moses, and led to his call to become the leader of his people. When Moses asked who was sending him to Pharaoh, the response came back: "I AM...."

In John 8:58, Jesus affirmed His divine nature by appropriating the divine name to Himself: "...before Abraham came to be, I AM." Whereupon the Jews tried to stone Him for blasphemy.

Christ the Redeemer is the burning bush. "I have come to light a fire on the earth!" (Luke 12:49). This saving fire of love descended upon the 120 apostles and disciples at Pentecost. It burns in the thorn bush of the Church until the New Jerusalem comes down from heaven. "The glory of God lights up that city," writes St. John. "And its lamp is the Lamb" (Revelation 21:23).

The Key of David. In ancient times when a city surrendered, the keys of the city gate were brought to the conqueror. The "power of the keys" was threefold in biblical understanding: over the entrance of the gate to admit or exclude; over the prison to punish or to condone; over the storehouse and treasury to feed and to reward. In Isaiah (22:22), Eliakim received the key to the house of David. Eliakim and his key is another Old Testament symbol of Christ the Messiah, of whom the angels said, "The Lord will give him the throne of David his father. He will rule over the house of Jacob forever and his reign will be without end."

Christ, the possessor of the keys, gave keys to St. Peter after the latter's confession of faith at Caesarea Philippi: "I will entrust to you the keys of the kingdom of heaven. Whatever you declare bound on earth shall be bound in heaven; whatever you declare loosed on earth shall be loosed in heaven" (Matthew 16:19). The key of David as an Old Testament symbol of Christ is also found at the end of the Bible, where the glorified and exalted Christ has received from His heavenly Father the key of David: "The holy One, the true, who wields David's key, who opens and no one can close, who closes and no one can open" (Revelation 3:7).

Each of these three symbols foreshadowed the Messiah, whose empty tomb on Easter morning symbolizes for us today His ultimate victory over sin and death.

> *Hail to the Victor, Jesus, conqueror of doubt! Hail to the Victor, Jesus, conqueror of fear! Hail to the Victor, Jesus, conqueror of death! Hail to the conquering Hero, winner for us of certainty, confidence and life everlasting! Alleluia!*

SEVEN

Jesus, Our Light and Life

The Lord is my light and my salvation,
of whom should I be afraid?

Psalm 27

The Gospel of St. John contains seven statements of the Lord, each beginning with the words, "I am..." In each of them, the Lord reveals one aspect of the relationship that exists between the Redeemer and the redeemed. "I am the vine... the good shepherd... the light... the way... the resurrection... the bread... the door." Let's look at a few of these images.

"I am the vine, you are the branches..." (John 15:5-6). We share the life of Christ! This is the profound meaning of Baptism – in His goodness and mercy, God changes us from creatures into children, daughters and sons whom He loves. This reality makes religion more than a code of conduct or a body of beliefs. Religion becomes the joyful, exciting relationship with the Divine Trinity that enables us to bear fruit in our lives, good works that reach even into eternity through Him who enables us to do all things.

"...I am the good shepherd. I know my sheep and my sheep know me..." (John 10:11-16). Without fangs, claws, sharp teeth, or speedy legs, sheep are helpless against their natural enemies. They also lack a clear sense of direction, and need around-the-clock care to stay out of harm's way.

Helpless and without direction is also a good description of humankind after the Fall. However, as our good shepherd, Jesus knows us and calls us by name. Our Good Shepherd has entrusted His Church into the care of other shepherds, our pastors. These shepherds are ready around the clock, and willing to lay down their lives if necessary. They care for the flock already in the fold, seek out wild sheep that don't recognize the shepherd's voice, and guide back to the fold any who wander away.

"I am the light of the world..." (John 8:12). Candles have burned on Catholic altars since the days of the catacombs. The light they produce reminds us of the One who promised, "No follower of mine shall ever walk in darkness..." Four qualities of light suggest four facets of the relationship we have with Christ.

First, light moving at unbelievable speed to penetrate every part of Creation. No wonder we say that Jesus is "God from God, Light from Light."

Second, light is necessary to sustain life, whether plant or animal. When Jesus said, "I am the Light," He was telling us that He is absolutely necessary for the life of our souls.

Third, light assures us of safety. Sin is like darkness, putting us in danger of hell and the power of the Evil One; but we who are Christ's followers will never walk in darkness.

Fourth, light brightens and cheers. Jesus our Light is joy for all ages. His presence gladdens, cheers, and encourages us.

"I am the resurrection and the life..." (John 11:35-36). What is the purpose of life? How can I know for sure that, when my body dies, the spirit that animates me will live on? No doubt searching questions such as these occupied the thoughts of our ancestors long before they could record them for our benefit. And yet, no human response – not instinct, not science, not philosophy – has provided a satisfactory answer. To these ultimate questions, Jesus Christ alone gives an answer that rings with its own authority: "I am the resurrection... whoever believes in me, though he should die, will come to life."

The proof that He could do this for us was His own glorious resurrection from the grave, an event that has been celebrated by

Christians ever since. Yes, our blessed assurance of life everlasting and of final victory over the grave comes from the Savior who proclaimed, "I am the resurrection."

> *Jesus, You are the Vine in whom we have our life.*
> *You are the loving Shepherd — wise, all knowing.*
> *Jesus, You are our Living Bread in sacrifice.*
> *You are the Light and Door, the right way showing.*
> *Jesus, You give us eternally love and life.*
> *You are God's Precious Son and our one true light.*

> *(hhs)*

EIGHT

Bread of Life

---

*"I am the bread of life... If anyone eats this bread he shall live
forever; the bread I will give is my flesh for the life of the world."*

John 6:48, 51

Biblical bread, the honest-to-goodness wheat bread like
Grandma used to bake, is different from the soggy, pasty,
tasteless white bread available in stores today, so "enriched" with
chemicals each wrapper should probably be stamped with the
Surgeon General's warning.

Eating Grandma's bread, perhaps with some fish cooked in
olive oil and a glass of wine, was a memorable experience. To the
ancients, bread was synonymous with life. When Jesus taught us to
pray for our material needs, He said it all in one petition: "Give us
this day our daily bread."

Breaking a loaf of bread was a rite observed at Jewish
meals. In the account of the multiplication of the loaves, Matthew,
Mark, and Luke all state the Jesus "blessed the loaves, broke them
and gave them to the disciples" to distribute to the people. Later,
Jesus chose this most common food of His time as a way to give
Himself to us. When He said, "I am the bread...", He was telling us
that just as food is necessary for the life and health of our bodies, so
His flesh in the Blessed Sacrament is necessary for the life and
health of our souls.

In all four Gospel accounts, Jesus broke the bread and gave
it to His disciples saying, "Take this and eat it; this is my body." It
was also by this action that the two Emmaus disciples came to

recognize Jesus on the evening of the Resurrection: "When he had seated himself with them to eat, he took bread, pronounced the blessing, then broke the bread and began to distribute it to them. With that their eyes were opened and they recognized him, whereupon he vanished from their sight" (Luke 24:30-31). Later that same evening the pair recounted to the Eleven "how they had come to know him in the breaking of the bread" (Luke 24:25).

What the first Christians called the Breaking of the Bread (see Acts 2:42, 46; 20:7, 11) is what we call today the Mass and Holy Eucharist. Jesus said it was His Body and His Blood. Not just a symbol or memorial, not just a reminder or a token, but His real Body and Blood. This reality is captured beautifully in *Lauda Sion,* a great Eucharistic hymn of St. Thomas Aquinas:

Bone pastor, panis vere,	Very Bread, Good Shepherd, tend us,
Iesu, nostri miserere:	Jesus, of Thy love befriend us,
Tu nos pasce, nos tuere:	Thou refresh us, Thou defend us,
Tu nos bona fac videre	Thy eternal goodness send us
In terra viventium.	In the land of life to see.
Tu, qui cuncta scis et vales;	Thou who all things sees and knows,
Qui nos pascis hic mortales;	Who on earth such food bestows,
Tuos ibi commensales,	Grant us with Thy Saints, though lowest,
Coheredes et sodales	Where the heavenly feast Thou showest,
Fac sanctorum civium.	Fellow-heirs and guests to be.

NINE

Marks of Christ's Humanity

————⟶•⟸————

Henceforth let no man trouble me;
for I bear on my body the marks of Jesus.

Galatians 7:17

In my "little black book," where I enter good ideas and holy thoughts that come my way, I have notes from a sermon given by a Minnesota pastor way back in 1974. At the time, I remember thinking, "Holy smoke, this can be developed into half a dozen sermons!"

All of us have been vitally affected by experiences in our lives, people we have known, places we have been. We say that these experiences, people and places have "left their mark" upon our lives. In his sermon, this Minnesota pastor listed six such significant impressions upon the life of Christ: the mark of the stable, the mark of the carpenter ship, the mark of the wilderness, the mark of the synagogue, the mark of the cross, and the mark of the empty tomb.

Our imitation of Christ is of course affected most by our own experiences. And yet, we also benefit by reflecting upon and imitating the example of Jesus at the crucial turning points and milestones of His own life.

The Mark of the Stable. So familiar are we with the story of the first Silent Night in Bethlehem, and so inextricably linked is this story with our own childhood memories, that most of us probably don't think about the scandal of God being born in a stable. However, the birth in the stable externalized dramatically what St. Paul described in his famous passage about the Emptying in the letter to the

Philippians: "Though he was in the form of God, Jesus did not deem equality with God something to be grasped at. Rather, he emptied himself and took the form of a slave, being born in the likeness of men."

The mark of the stable, the mark of The Emptying, followed Jesus throughout His public ministry. He mentioned once that the foxes have dens, the birds have nests, but the Son of Man had nowhere to lay His head. Dumb animals and simple shepherds were the first to celebrate His birth. It's not strange, then, is it, that He seemed so much more at home among the "little people" – the handicapped, the poor and the outcast.

Jesus was obedient to the Father's plan from the stable to the cross, never more explicitly than on the night of His agony when He prayed, "Not my will but yours be done." So far was He from grasping His equality with the Father that He made His own the psalmist's complaint: "My God, my God, why have you forsaken me?"

Having taken the form of a slave and been born in Bethlehem's stable, Jesus also died like a slave in a disgraceful, criminal execution. But the mark of the stable was turned into glory because "God highly exalted him and bestowed on him the name above every other name... so that at Jesus' name every knee must bend... and every tongue proclaim... Jesus Christ is Lord!"

Almighty God, we have been redeemed from the old life of sin by our baptism into the death and resurrection of your Son, Jesus Christ. Grant that we may be renewed in your Holy Spirit to live in justice and true holiness. We ask this through Christ our Lord. Amen.

TEN

Mark of the Carpenter Shop

———◦———

*"Is not this the carpenter, the son of Mary
and brother of James and Joses and Judas and Simon,
and are not his sisters here with us?"
And they took offense at him.*

Mark 6:3

Jesus spent thirty years in quiet growth and development; "the hidden life," as devotional writers are wont to call it. The years in Nazareth centered in the home and carpenter shop of His mother Mary and His stepfather Joseph.

Later, when He returned to Nazareth to teach in its synagogue, Jesus' fellow townspeople were filled with amazement. "Where did this man get such wisdom and miraculous powers?" they asked. "Isn't this the carpenter's son?" Other manuscripts render the second question, "Isn't this the carpenter, the son of Mary?" The latter rendering would suggest that Jesus was remembered as a skilled woodworker Himself.

One of the wood products that Joseph and Jesus would have fashioned for the farmers and teamsters of Galilee would have been yokes for teams of oxen. When our Lord said, "Take my yoke upon you and learn from me, for my yoke is easy and my burden light," this metaphor sprang from His own life's experience.

The years in the carpenter shop left their mark on the human Christ in more basic ways than on His reputation and in His speech. His lifestyle was very ordinary, enabling Him to identify so much with the common people of His time. The everyday routine of the carpenter shop probably prompted Him to appreciate more than most the beauty outdoors – birds, lilies, fields, skies.

His familiarity with the Law and the Prophets, His habit of attendance at the synagogue and the temple, suggest that the Nazareth years were years in which Jesus as a man grew in the grace of His Father, slowly, steadily, unremarkably. That's the way spiritual growth will usually occur in us, too.

True progress quietly and persistently moves along without notice.
Francis de Sales

ELEVEN

Mark of the Wilderness

—————◦—————

Then Jesus was led by the Spirit out into the wilderness to be tempted by the devil. He fasted for forty days and forty nights, after which he was very hungry, and the tempter came...

Luke 4:2

This gospel passage is frightening. Think of it, Emmanuel – the sinless Son of God – being tempted! But tempted He was, with the idea of being a material and political Messiah having all the accompanying human perks. The encounter with the Evil One was an exhausting struggle. When it was over, "angels appeared and looked after him."

Of all the experiences that left their mark on our Lord Jesus, the wilderness encounter is perhaps the one with which we can most identify. The devil offered Jesus three goodies that tempt us still.

The first temptation was *pleasure*. "Command these stones to turn into bread..." Satisfy yourself, Jesus. Why be hungry, why work? You have the power to make a life of ease for yourself. Take care of Number One. Eat, drink and be merry.

The second temptation was *popularity*. "Throw yourself down" from the high temple wall. The angels will see that you don't hurt yourself, Jesus. And the crowds will love it. A few showy tricks like that and you'll have a real following.

The third temptation was *power*. "All these kingdoms I will bestow upon you if you prostrate yourself in homage before me." Sell me your soul, Jesus, and I'll see that you really get ahead. Profit's the name of the game. Be a go-getter.

When you think about it, our temptations tend heavily to pleasure, popularity or power. Jesus showed us how to overcome them. By prayer, self-discipline and the Holy Scriptures, Jesus came out of the wilderness the victor.

Since the fourth century, Christians have practiced prayer, fasting, and almsgiving as a means to this kind of self-discipline, particularly during the season of Lent, when newcomers to the faith were making final preparations to receive Baptism, Confirmation and First Communion at Easter. Pope Paul VI, who first implemented the reforms brought about by the Second Vatican Council, issued the documents that set the stage for the restoration of these ancient spiritual practices.

However, Pope Paul VI saw a world in which almost half the people are hungry and many were starving. Fasting was a permanent condition for these millions. The pope saw a Third World in which people seldom have meat. Laws of fasting and abstinence were a cruel joke for these people; so on February 17, 1966, the pope did away with the *laws* of fasting and abstinence. However, he did not do away with the *practice*. And so on Ash Wednesday and Good Friday we are still asked to fast and abstain (those between the ages of 21 and 59), and to abstain from meat on the Fridays of Lent (those older than 14).

The spiritual exercises of prayer, fasting, and almsgiving are conducive to spiritual growth throughout life. Private devotions like daily Scripture reading, praying before the Blessed Sacrament, or periodically making the Stations of the Cross can better dispose one to serve the Lord. Abstinence, whole or partial, from alcohol, television, tobacco, or sweets would be a healthy practice for most of us. Offering your time and talent as a volunteer to help the sick, shut-in, unemployed, hungry, or homeless is the best kind of almsgiving.

Compared with those who struggle for existence in the Third World, we have an embarrassing abundance of riches. May the Lord enlarge our hearts to see the good He would have us do with all He has entrusted into our care.

> *Lord, make me an instrument of your peace.*
> *where there is hatred, let me sow love;*

when there is injury, pardon;
where there is doubt, faith;
where there is despair, hope;
where there is darkness, light;
and where there is sadness, joy.

Grant that I may not so much seek
to be consoled, as to console;
to be understood, as to understand;
to be loved, as to love.

For it is in giving that we receive,
it is in pardoning that we are pardoned,
and it is in dying [to ourselves] that we are born to
eternal life.

TWELVE

Mark of the Synagogue

He came to Nazareth where he had been brought up, and went into the synagogue on the Sabbath day as he usually did...

Luke 4:16

In the heart of the oldest section of Nazareth is the town synagogue, where it is believed Jesus learned to read and write and studied the Law and the Prophets. "Synagogue" means a bringing together, an assembly hall. The mark of the Jewish synagogue is seen again and again in Jesus' life and teaching.

St. Matthew records several times that Jesus "taught in their synagogues." St. John's account of Jesus' hearing before the high priest on the night of His Passion includes the Lord's assertion, "I have spoken openly... I have always taught in the synagogue... where all the Jews meet together."

At least one of Jesus' early miracles, the exorcism of the demoniac reported by Mark and Luke, occurred in a synagogue. But more significant by far is our Lord's total familiarity with the religious laws and customs of His people, both the letter and the spirit of those laws. He loved the synagogue and the temple, He loved His people and limited His own ministry to the children of Israel.

The mark of the synagogue was never more poignantly displayed than in the Holy Week incident when Jesus came within sight of Jerusalem. He wept over the city and its nation, doomed to destruction for failing to recognize the message of salvation.

Successor to the synagogue is the visibly organized church. Despite its human weaknesses and imperfections, it too is the assembly of God's people. In it the ministry of Christ continues. The mark of the Church should be on us just as the mark of the synagogue was on the Savior.

> *The Church's one foundation is Jesus Christ her Lord,*
> *She is His new creation by water and the Word.*
> *From heaven He came and sought her to be His holy bride;*
> *With His own blood He bought her, and for her life He died.*
>
> *She is from every nation, yet one o'er all the earth;*
> *Her charter of salvation, one Lord, one faith, one birth;*
> *One holy Name she blesses, partakes one holy food,*
> *And to one hope she presses, with every grace endued.*

THIRTEEN

Mark of the Cross

*But far be it from me to glory except in the cross
of our Lord Jesus Christ, by which the world has been
crucified to me, and I to the world.*

Galatians 6:14

We have been considering those places and experiences in Jesus' life that left their mark on His humanity. We are helped in our own lives by knowing how our Lord behaved in these situations.

The mark of the cross was on Jesus Christ long before He went to Calvary. In the Temple, before Jesus was even two months old, Simeon and Anna predicted grim things about Him, "destined to be the downfall and the rise of many in Israel." As Jesus grew into boyhood, into His teens and into manhood, He became increasingly familiar with the prophecies of Isaiah. We marvel at the detail with which Isaiah (and other prophets too) foretold the sufferings of the Passion.

From the day of Peter's confession and the conferral of the keys, Jesus began to tell His disciples that He would have to go to Jerusalem, suffer many things, be killed and be raised the third day. Two days before the final Passover He reminded them that "the Son of Man is to be handed over to be crucified."

The mark of the cross became literal and physical on Good Friday and now identifies even the glorified body of the risen Christ. After Easter the Lord invited Thomas to touch the wounds in His hands and on His side. I believe we shall see these glorious trophies after our own resurrection.

The lesson for us from the mark of the cross is put plainly in Luke 9:23. "Whoever wishes to be my follower must deny his very self, *take up his cross each day,* and follow in my steps. Whoever would save his life will lose it, and whoever loses his life for my sake will save it." The mark of the cross is a vital sign of discipleship.

Some years ago Senator Mark Hatfield of Oregon spoke at the annual New York Prayer Breakfast, and recounted a conversation he had had with Mother Teresa of Calcutta. He had asked her whether she ever experienced discouragement in her work with the poor and hungry. How could she measure her success, when the need was so great?

"God has not called me to be successful," replied Mother Teresa. "He has called me to be faithful."

We don't say enough about faithfulness these days, but fidelity to our calling is at the heart of taking up one's cross for Christ. The Lord asks us to be faithful to our work, our spouses, our families, our neighbors, our beliefs, our country and our God. "God is faithful," the Scriptures tell us. The mark of the cross is seen on us to the extent that we are able to mirror that fidelity in good times and in bad.

> *Great is Thy faithfulness, O God my Father.*
> *There is no shadow of turning with Thee.*
> *Thou changest not, Thy compassions, they fail not;*
> *As Thou hast been, Thou forever will be.*

> *Great is Thy faithfulness, great is Thy faithfulness!*
> *Morning by morning new mercies I see.*
> *All I have needed Thy hand hath provided;*
> *Great is Thy faithfulness, Lord, unto me!*
>
> Thomas Chisholm, 1923

FOURTEEN

Mark of the Open Tomb

*Now on the first day of the week Mary Magdalene came
to the tomb early, while it was still dark, and saw that
the stone had been taken away from the tomb.*

John 20:1

Everything else that happened to Jesus Christ pales before the power of His resurrection. All the other events and places that left their mark on His humanity, from the crib to the cross, are as nothing compared to the open tomb on Easter morning.

The earlier marks were very human: the birth in Bethlehem, the hidden life in Nazareth, the test in the wilderness, the service in the synagogue, the death on the cross. But when He burst forth from the tomb, the divinity of the God-Man took over.

Post-resurrection gospels struggle with words to describe Christ's glorified body. Apostles and other witnesses recognized Him as truly the Lord they had known, but His coming and going and manner and mien were now different. St. Paul told his readers that, in our own resurrection, our bodies are going to be glorified in a similar way.

Divinity radiates from Christ's open tomb even more in that the resurrection is the very heart of God's saving work. It's the ultimate statement that salvation isn't something man or woman can do; it's the work of God. The same must be said of the renewal of our lives and the renewal of the Church, our religious priority in recent years. It isn't something we do; we must open ourselves up to God's action in us.

As is so often the case, St. Paul has a passage that sums up what Lent and Easter should mean and do for us. His epistle to the Romans tells us what the mark of the tomb calls us to: "If we have died with Christ, we believe that we are also to live with him. We know that Christ, once raised from the dead, will never die again; death has no more power over him. His death was death to sin, once for all; his life is life for God. In the same way you must consider yourselves dead to sin but alive for God in Christ Jesus" (Romans 6:8-11).

Take my life and let it be consecrated, Lord, to Thee.
   Take my moments and my days; let them flow in ceaseless praise.
Take my hands, and let them move at the impulse of Thy love.
   Take my feet, and let them be swift and beautiful for Thee.

Take my will, and make it Thine; it shall be no longer mine.
   Take my heart, it is Thine own; it shall be Thy royal throne.
Take my love, my Lord, I pour at Thy feet its treasure store.
   Take myself, and I will be ever, only, all for Thee.

Frances Havergal, 1873

FIFTEEN

Mountains of the Lord – Part One

It shall come to pass in the latter days that the mountain of the house of the LORD shall be established as the highest of the mountains, and shall be raised above the hills; and all the nations shall flow to it.

Isaiah 2:2

The central events in the life of Jesus occurred on the mountains of Palestine, from the Mountain of Temptation, where our Lord was tested by the evil one, to Mount Calvary, where He finished our salvation on the cross. There are six elevations, to be exact. These elevations are not very high – not like the Rockies or Appalachians. But they loom over the plains of Palestine and over the Jordan Valley, and loom large in the life of Jesus. Over the next two days, we will explore each of these six mountaintops.

The Mount of Temptation. After fasting forty days and nights, Jesus was weak and hungry. Satan offered Him instant comfort and fame, and when rebuffed, transported Jesus to the mountaintop, where the evil one offered the Lord instant power. "All these kingdoms I will bestow on you, if you prostrate yourself in homage before me." Jesus' resistance teaches us some important lessons on what it is to be human. It is to have one need that surpasses any other – more than comfort, more than fame, more than power. It is the need for God Himself, to be in tune with the hymn of all creation that gives homage to God and adores Him alone.

The human Jesus, our Brother, was tempted exactly as we are tempted. He was victorious on the mountaintop, where angels came and ministered to Him. And, though Jesus Himself resisted temptation, the Gospels tell us that He has endless compassion for those who fall.

Mount Tabor. Tabor was like Camelot for Peter, James and John; it was on this mountain where the Lord was transfigured in the very presence of these three apostles. For "one brief shining moment," their human eyes saw the divine Christ in all His glory. It was a vision they would need to overcome the trials-by-fire that lay ahead of them.

The Christian life alternates between valley and vision. We, too, need our mountaintop experiences, something to put a glow into our daily struggle, to cast a halo about our inner conflicts, and to renew the meaning and purpose of our baptismal vows. These mountaintop experiences come in many different forms: a fervent feast-day liturgy, an answered prayer, a walk in the woods, a conversation with a good friend, or a homily that strikes a chord. In those moments, we can say, "Lord, it's good to be here."

Mount Zion. The hill on which Jerusalem is built, and where the temple stood, is at the heart of Israel. "I myself installed my king on Zion, my holy mountain," the psalmist quotes God as saying (Psalm 2:6). Like every true Israelite, Jesus loved Mount Zion, and must have joined the other pilgrims in song as He went with His parents up to the feast. "I rejoiced when they said to me, 'Let us go up to the house of the Lord'" (Psalm 122:1). However, it was also in this place where Jesus experienced sharp confrontations with the Jewish leaders. It was out of the Temple in Jerusalem that Jesus drove the moneychangers, and ultimately predicted its destruction.

For the Christian, it is not this earthly Jerusalem but "the Jerusalem above" that is our mother (Galatians 4:26). The end of our earthly pilgrimage is "Mount Zion and the city of the living God, the heavenly Jerusalem" (Hebrews 12:22). It is here that we will see the Lamb of God who takes away the sins of the world. May He have mercy on us and grant us peace.

SIXTEEN

Mountains of the Lord – Part II

—————

*And after he had dismissed the crowds, he went up on the mountain
by himself to pray. When evening came, he was there alone...*

Matthew 14:23

Yesterday we explored three of the six mountains that were
significant to the earthly life and ministry of Jesus: the
Mountain of Temptation, Mount Tabor, and Mount Zion. These
three mountains were formative in private life of Christ, particularly
in the years prior to His public ministry. The next three mountains
have a strong connection to the public ministry of Jesus – and especially the events surrounding His Passion and Death.

Mount of the Beatitudes. In 1956, I was able to visit the beautiful
eight-sided chapel that dominates the shoreline in Galilee in the
vicinity of the likely site of the famous "Sermon on the Mount." On
each of the chapel walls, a stained glass window depicts one of the
eight "blessed" pronounced by the Lord.

Just like Moses, who spoke to the Jewish people on Mount
Sinai in the Arabian Desert, the "New Moses" preached His most
famous sermon early in His public ministry, from the side of a
mountain sloping up from the shores of the Sea of Galilee. By His
own admission, the New Moses had come not to abolish the law,
but to fulfill it. He made even greater demands on His followers
than Moses did – and yet He also liberally bestowed the justice and

grace needed to meet these demands.

Mount of Olives. The fifth of the six significant mountains in the life of Christ stands immediately to the east of Jerusalem, separated from the city by a deep depression called the Kidron Valley. At one time, olive orchards covered the hillside; the elevation is known as Mount of Olives, or Mount Olivet.

At the foot of the Mount of Olives is the Garden of Gethsemane, where the Lord prayed until beads of sweat formed upon His brow, that the bitter cup might pass from Him. At the summit of the mountain is the site of the Ascension, from which Christ the Victor returned to His Father. Thus Mount Olivet is the location of both sorrowful and glorious mysteries in our redemption story.

Mount Calvary. The site of the Crucifixion was not a real mountain, nor even much of a hill. *Golgotha,* Hebrew for "place of the skull," was a natural elevation of some sort, since executions took place along the main roads leading to or from the city so the public might see what was in store for malefactors. Since the fourth century, the hill of Calvary has been enclosed in the eastern end of the Church of the Holy Sepulcher.

Calvary was not an inspiring, uplifting scene. Crucifixion was cruel and bloody. Criminals were stripped naked before having stakes driven into their flesh, then left to slowly bleed to death. The loss of blood produced a blazing thirst; each breath was torture. This "emblem of suffering and shame," however, was a stupendous success from a spiritual perspective. It was here that Christ attained atonement, reconciliation and forgiveness for us by humbling Himself, becoming obedient even to death on a cross. Scriptures tell us, "because of this, God greatly exalted him and bestowed on him the name that is above every name, that at the name of Jesus every knee should bend and every tongue proclaim to the glory of God the Father that Jesus Christ is Lord" (Philippians 2:10).

In 1913, George Bennard of Albion, Michigan penned what is arguably one of the best-loved hymns, commemorating the instrument of torture that has become the symbol of our greatest hope. In the final verse, Bennard penned the resolution of true Christians in every time and place:

To the old rugged cross I will ever be true
Its shame and reproach gladly bear,
Then He'll call me someday to my home far away
Where His glory forever I'll share!

Yes, I'll cherish that old rugged cross
Till my trophies at last I lay down.
I will cling to the old rugged cross,
And exchange it someday for a crown.

Section Three

Hope in the Spirit

SEVENTEEN

An Invisible Wind

*"And in the last days it shall be, God declares,
that I will pour out my Spirit upon all flesh..."*

Acts 2:17

When I was nine and in the third grade, in the spring of 1933, I got a kite for my birthday. The packet contained the frame of light wood, purple paper to cover the frame, and string to tie the assembly together. What the packet didn't contain was a tail. For the kite to fly straight and high, it needs some kind of rudder or tail.

My mother knotted together some pieces of cloth, and my dad tied them to the bottom of the kite. After several runs and attempts at launching, my purple kite had its maiden flight. The wind – the unseen force – lifted the kite into the sky. When you think about it, the wind brings a kite to fullness.

Jesus Himself compared the work of the Holy Spirit to the wind. "The wind blows where it will. You hear the sound it makes, but you do not know where it comes from or where it goes. So it is with everyone begotten of the Spirit" (John 3:8).

The first public manifestation of the Holy Spirit in the Church and in the world was at Pentecost in the form of wind (Acts 2:2). In Acts 2:1-4, we are told that the change worked in the apostles and other disciples was both dramatic and sudden. Like the invisible wind lifting the kite into the air, the Spirit of God ignited the hearts of the disciples and gave wing to the new Church. In the Pentecost event, the Spirit transformed the fear and confusion of the Twelve into understanding, enthusiasm and joy over the task they were about to begin.

Other times, God works more quietly, gently, and softly. He revealed Himself to Elijah as a "tiny whispering sound" after the earthquake and fire had passed (see 1 Kings 19:9-18). The Holy Spirit comes to us in many ways: in the preaching of God's Word, in prayer, in the Holy Absolution ("God the father of mercies... has sent the Holy Spirit among us for the forgiveness of sins..."), and in the Eucharist ("Grant that we who are nourished by His Body and Blood may be filled with His Holy Spirit and become one body, one spirit in Christ.").

Only six words are dedicated to the Spirit in the Apostle's Creed (only five in the original Greek, four in the Latin version), which adds credence to the idea that the Spirit is the "forgotten Person" of the Blessed Trinity. However, the New Testament speaks fondly of the Holy Spirit. Jesus called this Third Person by the revealing name of Paraclete, which is translated in many ways: Advocate, Intercessor, Friend, Helper, Consoler, Comforter. He also called the Spirit of Truth who teaches, witnesses, demonstrates the errors of the world, and gives glory to Christ.

The sacred writers John, Paul and Peter all attest that the Scriptures are holy because they have been written under the inspiration of the Holy Spirit. The Spirit dwells in the Church and in the hearts of the faithful as in a temple; through the Spirit, the Church is guided into the fullness of truth and given a unity of fellowship and service. The New Testament ends (Revelations 21:17) with the magnificent picture of the Spirit leading the Church to perfect union with her spouse, the Lord Jesus: "The Spirit and the bride say, 'Come!'"

> *May the wind of Pentecost continue to blow in our day and time! Come, Holy Spirit, give life and direction to our journey together as the People of God!*

EIGHTEEN

Images of the Spirit

...the Holy Spirit, through whom the living voice of the Gospel rings out in the Church - and through her in the world - leads believers to the full truth, and makes the Word of Christ dwell in them in all its richness.

CCC 79

A simile is a figure of speech that compares unlike things for purposes of clarity or color. Jesus the Divine Teacher often used similes. He said, for instance, the kingdom of heaven is like a mustard seed... like yeast mixed with three measures of wheat... like a net thrown into the sea... like a treasure buried in a field.

Since the Holy Spirit is divine, infinite, eternal, and invisible, and since all these are beyond our human experiences, Christian writers have resorted to simile to describe the Spirit to us. To what may the Holy Spirit be likened?

The Spirit is like the wind.

St. Luke, in the Acts of the Apostles, describes the coming of the Holy Spirit as a noise "like a strong wind blowing." Jesus said (John 3:8) that those born of the Spirit are like the wind too. One thinks also of Elijah's encounter with God (1 Kings 19:12) in the soft, tiny, whispering sound.

The Spirit is like fire.

Acts 2:1-4 records how the 120 disciples crowded into the upper room saw "tongues as of fire" settling on the heads of those assembled when the Spirit came. In a famous sermon, Bishop Griffin of Columbus, Ohio, compared the Spirit-filled apostles to the old-fashioned matches that exploded into flame by friction. Similarly, opposition and persecution made fiery missionaries out of the cowards of Good Friday.

The Spirit is like the rain.

In one of his sermons, St. Cyril of Jerusalem reminded his hearers that at Jacob's Well in Samaria Jesus called the grace of the Holy Spirit "living water." He explained, "Water comes down as rain and affects every living creature in its own way."

The Spirit is like sunshine.

Another Church Father, St. Basil the Great, wrote on his treatise of the Holy Spirit: "Like the sunshine which permeates all the atmosphere and yet is enjoyed by each person as if it were for him alone, so the Spirit pours forth grace in full measure, sufficient for all yet present as though exclusively to each who receives him."

Wind, fire, rain, sun… these are very elemental things in our lives. Human life would be impossible without them. Holy Spirit, once again blow, warm, pour, and shine upon us with gifts of grace.

NINETEEN

When God Is Distant

Every question possesses a power that does not lie in the answer.

Elie Wiesel
Nobel Prize winner and concentration camp survivor

Out of the notorious Auschwitz concentration camp comes a story of a group of Jewish inmates who one day put God on trial, charging Him with cruelty and betrayal. In their circumstances they could find no excuse for the evil horrors they were experiencing as individuals and as a people. So, after considerable argumentation, they found God guilty and, presumably, worthy of death. As the Law required, the rabbi solemnly announced the verdict.

Then the rabbi looked up and said that the trial was over. It was time for them to begin evening prayer. And they did.

For thousands of years before the Incarnation – precisely how long, we do not know – the human race groped in darkness. As St. Paul wrote in the first chapter of Romans, God was visible and knowable from the things He made, but the perverse minds and weakened wills of mankind kept seekers from finding Him.

Finally, when the "fullness of time" had come, God changed His hiding place. In the still of a winter's night, He slipped down from heaven into a manger. The Almighty God who "does not dwell in sanctuaries made by human hands" slept in the hay, the guardian of Israel who "neither sleeps nor slumbers." In the words of the Apostle John, the Word came to dwell among us. The wonder, the beauty, the truth of Christmas is that our search is over. God is with us.

Nevertheless, all of us have felt His absence at one time or another – in times of pain, in times of change, in times of trauma. Maybe we didn't feel the hopelessness of Auschwitz, but we've had our doubts and misgivings about the Gospel. And the absence of God can cripple us spiritually and emotionally for a while. Yet we know that we will discover God again in acts of love, generosity, support and healing coming to us from Jesus, often through the actions of others who are inspired by Him.

Our Lord's great Eucharistic discourse on the Bread of Life, recorded in the sixth chapter of John's Gospel, was too much for some of the disciples. They just couldn't believe what Jesus was promising, and they broke off from His company. Jesus then said to the Twelve, "Do you want to leave me too?"

Peter answered for them all: "Lord, to whom shall we go? You have the words of eternal life!" That kind of faith and that answer has to be ours also. It will see us through the most difficult of times, because the reality is that God is the only real, constant source of all that is good, true and beautiful. Like those Jews who tried God and found Him wanting, to whom else would we go?

TWENTY

Seeing with Eyes of Faith

———

Jesus said to him, "Have you believed because you have seen me?
Blessed are those who have not seen and yet believe."

John 20:29

The liturgy of the Feast of the Transfiguration of the Lord, celebrated each year on August 6, takes us to that mountaintop in
Galilee where Peter, James, and John for one brief and shining
moment saw Jesus in all His majesty and glory. The three men were
overcome with awe, then brought quickly back to their earthbound
pilgrimage (Luke 9:28-36). Thirty years later, Peter wrote: "we
were eye witnesses of his sovereign majesty... while we were in his
company on the holy mountain" (2 Peter 1:19).

The earthly ministry of Jesus was full of signs and miracles
– there are seven remarkable events recorded in the early chapters
of John's Gospel alone. The first was the changing of water into
wine at the wedding at Cana. The second sign also took place in
Galilee – the healing of the official's son (see John 4:46-54). The
uniqueness of the second sign is the fact that it was a "long-
distance" cure. Jesus does not see the boy, does not touch him and
does not speak to him. Jesus' word ALONE gave life to this child,
who was "near death."

Our Lord was critical of the Jewish eagerness to witness
miracles. "Unless you people see signs and wonders, you will not
believe." In the longer Gospel account of Jesus' temptation in the
desert, twice He rejected the suggestion of the Evil One to work a
miracle. Our present generation also has a great fondness for such
signs. Even questionable reports of strange happenings, visions,
"inner locutions" and apparitions attract thousands quickly and

consistently.

Miracles do have their efficacy, but they are not to be overly esteemed. They are important if their deeper meaning is understood. What is more important is to stand open and receptive to the life-giving power of Jesus' Word.

> *Holy Spirit, move among us! Renew, restore, rejuvenate.*
> *Through the Word who dwells among and within us,*
> *Make us ever mindful of Your presence,*
> *And of the One who came to restore us into fellowship with the Father.*
> *Through Christ Our Lord, Amen.*

TWENTY-ONE

Wounded Healer

*But he was wounded for our transgressions, he was
bruised for our iniquities; upon him was the chastisement
that made us whole, and with his stripes we are healed.*

Isaiah 53:5

In May 1999, the *Detroit Free Press* ran a front-page article about Bishop Keith Symons, former head of the Diocese of Palm Beach, Florida. Bishop Symons resigned in 1998 after admitting that he had molested five young men 30 to 35 years ago. A native of the Upper Peninsula, Bishop Symons returned to Michigan.

The following year, with the permission of Bishop Mengling and my approval, too, Bishop Symons conducted a day of recollection for a small group of adults at the St. Francis Retreat Center in DeWitt. A self-appointed vigilante group based in Springfield, Illinois got wind of this and notified the media in Michigan and Florida that Bishop Symons was back into public ministry.

Three things must be said about these events.

First, the admissions of Bishop Symons have to do with actions committed more than thirty years ago. He has long since repented of them, been forgiven, and made reparation for them. Thirty years of amendment of life and commendable service in the priesthood and episcopate should be of some account.

Through my family members in Florida, I have known Keith Symons for more than a quarter of a century, when he was a priest and my parents and sisters were parishioners in the Diocese of St. Petersburg. Since he became a bishop in 1981 I got to know him even better and visited with him often. I was surprised by the charges he admitted to, but am certain of the genuineness of his conversion.

Secondly, the decision to allow Bishop Symons to return to pastoral ministry on a limited scale was not made casually. The Holy Father's representative in the U.S., the nuncio in Washington, was consulted, as were the bishops of Florida and the professional people who have been working with him.

Third, I take exception to the headlines that referred only to "a fallen cleric," "disgraced cleric," and "tainted bishop." I think there should have been included "a wounded healer." The late Henri Nouwen, author of thirty books on spirituality and prayer, had among his early titles one called *The Wounded Healer*. In it he said that ministers today are called to identify the suffering in their own hearts and make that recognition the starting point of their service.

For Nouwen, ministers must be willing to go beyond their professional, somewhat aloof role and leave themselves open as fellow human beings with the same wounds and sufferings as those they serve. In other words, we clergy and other ministers of souls can bring healing out of our own woundedness. Just as I have found that priests in recovery who belong to Alcoholics Anonymous are among the most effective in helping parishioners through personal problems, so I believe a bishop who has suffered as much as Keith Symons is likely to do an excellent job as a retreat director for adults.

Each of us carries within ourselves the wounds of wrong actions of the past – some of them inflicted upon us, others self-inflicted. May God grant us the courage and strength to look beyond our own hurts, to bring about a good greater than our pain.

God of grace and glory, who sees all,
who grieves every injustice,
and who longs to heal every injury,
hear our prayer.
We remember all those who have been
wounded by sin and cowardice.
Bring healing to those who long for wholeness.

And comfort to those who struggle in silence.
May your will be done here on earth, through us.
In the name of the One who died,
that sins might be forgiven, Amen.

(hhs)

TWENTY-TWO

A New Life to Come

"I am the resurrection and the life; whoever believes in me,
even if he dies, will live, and everyone who lives and
believes in me will never die."

John 11:25-26

The Smithsonian Institution and museums across the country are returning to Native American tribes the artifacts that archeologists took from Indian burial sites years ago. This is being done out of respect for the Indian dead, who believed they would need these things in another life in "the happy hunting ground."

This Indian belief in a life after death has its parallels in our tombstones, memorials, endowments, even in graffiti according to some psychologists. Humans do not want to be forgotten and refuse to believe that this life is all there is, that after a life of thought and choice we die like animals, that there is not a better life awaiting us where we will be reunited with loved ones.

Philosophers since ancient times have reasoned that there should be a life after death, but neither philosophy nor science is able to show us that there is. Jesus Christ alone gives the complete and satisfying answer to the question, "Is this all the life there is?"

Jewish believers had no clear revelation about the resurrection of the body, and Pharisees battled Sadducees over the issue (Matthew 22:23; Acts 23:6-10). Certainty about the resurrection of the body came with Jesus Christ, and the New Testament writers teach that all who have died will rise when Christ comes again in glory. "He who raised the Lord Jesus will raise us also with Jesus and bring us with you into his presence" (2 Corinthians 4:14).

This is going to be a universal resurrection. All the dead will rise again, the just unto glory and the unjust to judgment. Each will rise as the same person he or she was, in the same flesh made alive by the same spirit, but glorified and transformed with the new and unending life.

I was reminded of this reality again in 1973 at the library in Bamberg, Bavaria, I was shown a tenth-century miniature illustrating a biblical text. In the center was the baptismal font with a catechumen receiving the holy bath of Baptism from an elderly bishop. Three candidates for Baptism are waiting in line beyond the font, distinguished from the other persons in the picture by their dark-colored garments. This signified the old state of sin in which those who are not baptized live.

Those who have already passed through the bath of Baptism are marching upwards in jubilant procession. They are full of the splendor of holy rebirth and adorned in festive bright garments, their faces aglow with the halo of sanctity newly attained. A woman leads the procession of the newly baptized, and she approaches another woman who is adorned in an even more festive manner. This woman is identified as Mother Church, *Mater Ecclesia,* who offers the Eucharistic chalice to the newly baptized with her right hand. In her left hand she holds a staff adorned with a banner of victory. With the staff she points to the Cross, where the Lord now reigns in glory. The Latin inscription below the miniature painting reads: "These are the newborn lambs who have proclaimed the Alleluia. But a short time ago they came to the font; now they are filled with brightness."

This picture attests to the evangelization and initiation activity of the Church of a thousand years ago and to the joy of the Easter liturgy that centered on Baptism and New Life in "the Church's springtime." Because of this renewed emphasis on Easter as the baptismal feast, the faithful repeat their baptismal vows at the Masses on Easter.

Each time you repeat your baptismal vows – whether at Easter or at any other time of the year – may you do so with sincerity and truth. And may the vows you profess, which remind you of the new life that is yours in Christ, help you to be faithful to Him forever.

TWENTY-THREE

And Every Knee Shall Bow

Now thank we all our God, with hearts and hands and voices...

Martin Rinkart (1586-1649)

I once read an article in an ecumenical journal about the presence or absence of kneelers in churches. This is sometimes an issue among Catholics, particularly in light of the recent changes in the General Instruction of the Roman Missal (GIRM). The article pointed out that among the various Christian communions, the Orthodox are sometimes called "the Church standing," Roman Catholics are "the Church kneeling," and Protestants classified "the Church sitting."

What do these typical prayer postures tell us about the attitudes of those worshipping within those congregations? And what do these postures say about us as we assume them at various times in the Mass?

As one Orthodox priest told me, standing is considered the proper posture of a child of God coming into the presence of the Father. It denotes joyful and uninhibited praise. In the United States, we stand to show respect and our unity with one another. From the earliest days of the Church, standing has been associated with Christ's resurrection: We stand because we will one day share in that resurrected glory.

Kneeling, by contrast, is a posture of penitence and of adoration. This posture recognizes the indescribable "otherness" of God our Creator and Lord. Through the Incarnation He walked among us for a time; in the Real Presence, He continues to be among us still. The proper response to this kind of self-giving love is adoration – and so we kneel.

Sitting lends itself to a different kind of attentiveness – one that is waiting, ready, intent on learning. When we sit for the homily and for other parts of the Mass, we wait intently for whatever it is God wants to say to us through His ministers and especially through the presider. This, too, is an act of worship.

Each of the postures and gestures associated with worship, and particularly with participation in the Mass, are significant. Each of them, done with proper reverence and intent, help us to express and foster our faith. As we read in the General Instruction:

> *The external actions, movements, and posture of ... the people ought to draw things together in such a way that the entire celebration shines with beauty ad noble simplicity, that the true and full meaning of the different parts of the celebration is perceived, and that the participation of all is encouraged.... The uniformity of posture... is a sign of unity of the members of the Christian community gathered for the Sacred Liturgy; it both expresses and fosters the mind and the spiritual attitude of those present* (GIRM 42).

Holy Spirit, draw us together as one body.
> *As we stand rejoicing in the presence of the King,*
> *As we kneel adoring the Word made flesh among us,*
> *As we sit waiting expectantly for all you want to teach us.*
May our worship be pleasing in your sight,
> *And may our lives bear witness to the truth. Amen.*

(hhs)

Section Four

Growing Together as a People of God

TWENTY-FOUR

Four Signs of Spiritual Health

Every moment comes to us pregnant with a command from God,
only to pass on and plunge into eternity,
there to remain forever what we have made it.

Francis de Sales

Long ago when I was in seminary, one of my professors contended that there are four signs that indicate whether or not the Church is alive and healthy: the presence of martyrs, missionaries, monastics, and mystics. His words are as true today as when I first heard them more than fifty years ago.

The Church today is continually purified by the blood of her martyrs. In the century just past, Pope John Paul called for the identification of those who were killed for their faith in the concentration camps of Europe, the gulags of Siberia, the prisons of China, and the political turmoil of Latin America. They number in the hundreds of thousands, and many of these suffering saints will become known to us only in heaven.

Missionaries continue to devote their lives to the Church's growth and health. We Catholics can rejoice that we now number over *one billion members.* But even when Protestants and Orthodox are added to the total, two-thirds of the world's people are still non-Christians. So our work is still cut out for us.

Monasticism, meaning the Christian practice of taking vows to join a communal lifestyle as a prophetic witness to the world, has suffered setbacks in our time but still has a strong attraction for contemporary men and women. And mysticism, an experienced presence of God in which people have a deep sense of contact with

Him, is flourishing in charismatic and other "movements" that the Holy Father has encouraged all over the world.

As the People of God, we live out these four signs as well, each of us in a way appropriate to our situations. For example, not all are called to physical martyrdom. However, the Apostle Paul exhorts each of us to "present yourself a living sacrifice, holy and acceptable to God, which is your spiritual worship" (Romans 12:1). By offering up our trials, both great and small, we allow God to purify us from within. Even the elderly, the chronically ill and shut-ins who suffer in union with Christ are "witnesses" – the meaning of the Greek word from which we get the term "martyr."

Not all are called to travel thousands of miles to preach the Gospel in a distant land. Even so, Jesus tells us, "You are the light of the world.... Let your light so shine before men, that they may see your good works and give glory to your Father who is in heaven (Matthew 12:14, 16). Pope John Paul II has continued to empha-size what he calls a "New Evangelization." He is calling all of us to become evangelists for the new millennium. The pattern of action that typified the "old evangelization" – missionary work done by nuns, monks, priests, bishops, and other "professionals" – is inade-quate for this present age and culture. As in the early Church, everyone must share in the responsibility to maintain and spread the faith. People who show love, care and concern in the name of the Lord to neighbors, employees, fellow workers or fellow students testify to the God of love. They evangelize especially when others are ill, discouraged, or grieving.

Many people go their whole lives without setting foot in a monastery. And yet, we can experience a refreshing of the spirit by embracing the monastic practice of *"ora et labora"* (prayer and work). We can offer up the daily work of our hands, no matter how seemingly trivial, as a prayer to the God who gives us strength. Similarly, as we cultivate a habit of daily prayer, the abiding pres-ence of the Lord becomes very real to us. Saints throughout the ages discovered this mystical connection that enables us to remain faithful to our life's call.

Teresa of Avila, a sixteenth-century Spanish mystic and Carmelite reformer, understood the necessity of cultivating this spiritual connection. In one of her most well-known poems, she writes:

> *Let nothing trouble you, let nothing frighten you,*
> *All things pass away. God never changes.*
> *Patience obtains everything.*
> *Whoever possesses God wants for nothing.*
> *God alone suffices.*

TWENTY-FIVE

Unless ...

———➤●◄———

*"Unless the grain of wheat falls to the earth and dies, it remains
just a grain of wheat. But if it dies, it produces much fruit."*

John 12:24

Several times in the Gospels, Our Lord uses a small word to
signal an important contingency: "unless..." This word is a
contingency, an indicator that without the presence of one thing,
something else will not happen. In this passage, Jesus predicted His
passion, death and resurrection for the last time. His hour had come.
He was going to die and be buried in the earth, not against His will
but freely and out of obedient love. "I lay down my life in order to
take it up again. No one takes it from me, but I lay it down on my
own. I have the power to lay it down, and power to take it up again"
(John 10:18).

In several other places in the Gospels, Jesus uses the word
"unless" to remind His disciples of the task ahead of them. Each
instance involves a kind of "death" that is but a prelude to something greater. In Christ, death is never a real loss; it is but the necessary prelude to the greatest gain.

Unless you forgive.... You may recall how, in the Parable of the
Unforgiving Servant, the king in the story wrote off a huge debt of a
servant, who immediately put the heat on a second servant who owed
the first one a piddling amount. The angry king handed the first
servant over to the torturers. Our Lord's solemn warning is clear:

77

> *"My heavenly Father will treat you in exactly the same way unless each of you forgives his brother from the heart"* (Matthew 18:35).

The necessity of forgiveness is seen again in the Lord's Prayer, in which Jesus taught His disciples to pray, "And forgive us our trespasses, as we forgive those who trespass against us."

In the Sermon on the Mount, the words of the Lord's Prayer (Matthew 6:9-13) are followed immediately by these: "If you forgive others their transgressions, your heavenly Father will forgive you. But if you do not forgive others, neither will your Father forgive your transgressions" (6:14-15). We are required to imitate divine mercy if we ourselves wish to receive it.

Unless you grow in holiness... The Sermon on the Mount is the first of several major sermons quoted in Matthew's Gospel. The commentators agree that Matt 5:20 states the basic theme of what is the most famous sermon of all.

> *"Unless your holiness surpasses that of the scribes and Pharisees, you shall not enter the kingdom of God"* (Matthew 5:20).

The scribes were learned rabbis of the time, experts in the Law of Moses. The verses following this one (5:21-48) contrast the holiness or righteousness of the experts in the law and the better holiness or righteousness taught by Jesus. In the second major section of the sermon (6:1-18), Our Lord warns against the purely external holiness cultivated by the Pharisees, who were strict about the letter of the law, but they were lax about its real spirit. They took the front seats in synagogues, made a show of their benevolences, and prayed on the street corners; but sometimes they didn't take care of their aged parents.

We Catholics must guard against observing the letter and not the spirit of the law. Our religion has many external aspects, but we must see to it that our faith is solidly internal as well. Giving alms, praying and fasting, Jesus said, are useless if not done for the glory of God.

Unless you change... The disciples had just put a question to Jesus that had preoccupied their minds for some time: Who among them was to be the greatest in God's kingdom? Jesus put their speculations to rest quickly and succinctly.

> *"Unless you change and become like little children,*
> *you will not enter the kingdom of God"* (Matthew 18:3).

"Unless you change..." Change is another word for conversion. It means turning from one way of thinking and acting to another. For most of us, change is a task that never ends. There are always things that need improvement in our lives, even though we remain basically faithful to our baptismal vows. Anyone who thinks he or she has it made because of membership in the Catholic Church, or because he has "made the nine first Fridays" or because she tithes time, talent or treasure, or because he has a degree in theology or has been ordained a bishop tragically misunderstands the kingdom of God. That kingdom is for those who recognize that they have no right or claim to it but accept it as God's gift, just as a child accepts with implicit trust whatever his father offers.

TWENTY-SIX

The Be-Attitudes: Your Guide to Happiness

Happy the people whose God is the LORD!

Psalm 144:15

The eight Beatitudes have been described as our Lord's rules or laws for happiness. The word translated as "blessed" in our English New Testament and in the Catechism is *makarios* in the original Greek, meaning "happy." These beatitudes have been recast by some modern catechists as the "Be Attitudes." Corny, I know. However, they mean that there are eight attitudes we ought to strive to have in the depths of our very being in order to be truly happy: poverty in spirit, meekness, mercy, purity of heart, and so on.

For example, the second rule or law for happiness is that mourners will be comforted. The language here harkens back to the prophecy of Isaiah: "The spirit of the Lord is upon me, because the Lord has anointed me: He has sent me to bring glad tidings to the lowly... to comfort all who mourn" (Isaiah 61:1-2). Jesus quoted this passage at the outset of His Galilean ministry, when He preached on the Sabbath to His townsmen and relatives in the Nazareth synagogue.

Today when we speak of mourning, we generally refer to grief over someone's death. However, this is not the kind of sorrow our Lord had in mind when He spoke those words. How do we know? In the Gospel, when Jesus met death in the person of the daughter of Jairus, He makes a revealing comment: "The child is not dead. She is asleep" (Mark 5:39). He told the Twelve the same thing when He heard the sad news from Bethany: "Lazarus our friend is sleeping" (John 11:11). Statements like these led St. Paul to write that we should not grieve over those who are asleep like people who have no hope. "For if we believe that Jesus died and rose again, so too will God, through Jesus, bring with him those who have fallen asleep" (1 Thessalonians 4: 14).

Our convictions about death are based on our hope in Christ Jesus, our trust in His promises, and on the certainty that comes from His resurrection. The Office of the Dead, our Church's official prayer on the day of burial, states, "It was easier for Jesus to raise the dead to life than it is for us to arouse those who are sleeping." That is why I say to you and believe that our dead are only asleep. Jesus will raise them up on that Great and Glorious Day of the Judgment, and we are going to see them again in glory.

That being the case, the words of the Beatitude must have a wider application. For example, there is very little mourning over sin in modern life, but there is plenty of mourning among people who have a wrong scale of values. There are people who mourn their lack of brains, lack of beauty, lack of money, lack of position. Jesus teaches that these values have very little to do with true, spiritual, lasting happiness.

In reality, happiness may be had even in the midst of great suffering or sorrow. Jesus never became sour; if we accept the hard realities of life and bear with them, with the help of divine grace, we won't either. Happiness is not an end. It is a result.

The only ones among you who will be really happy
are those who will have sought and found how to
serve.

Albert Schweitzer

TWENTY-SEVEN

Blind Eyes Made to See

*Amazing grace, how sweet the sound
that saved a wretch like me!
I once was lost, but now am found;
was blind, but now I see.*

John Newton (1725-1807)

Every year, hundreds of men and women within our 93 diocesan parishes prepare for reception into the Church at Easter through the Rite of Christian Initiation of Adults (RCIA). This process, which was the practice of the ancient Church and restored to the Church of our time in 1972, includes an intensive time of Lenten preparation for both catechumens (the "elect" to be baptized at the Vigil) and candidates (previously baptized Christians to be received fully into the Catholic Church). The Scrutinies of Lent include special prayers and an exorcism over the elect, that all spiritual darkness and blindness may be dissipated by the gift of faith in Christ.

At the Second Scrutiny, we hear the account of the man born blind (John 9:1-41), one of the seven signs of the self-revelation of Jesus. The blind man is an intriguing figure: courageous and intelligent, countering with devastating success every blow cast his way by the critics of Jesus.

It is difficult for a sighted person to fully appreciate what it must have been like for the man born blind to see his world for the first time. And yet, each of us knows what it means to walk in darkness from time to time, to be blinded by sin. All sin harms the soul; choosing to continue in that sin without repentance leads to spiritual blindness, and ultimately spiritual death. Seven of these infectious habits are called "deadly sins."

Pride, or the belief that one is the center of the universe, is the deadliest source of sin. Only God can be the true center. True humility, the antidote of pride, involves knowing who you are and being content in that, rather than trying to be (or seem to be) more.

Greed, the second most potent source of our sinning, is a love of money or possessions over people. While it is not inherently wrong to possess things, it is a dead end. In the last analysis, it is people who make us happy, not things.

Lust, to early philosophers, described any appetite or desire. One might lust for power – or for a sailboat or a Picasso. In this day and age, "lust" almost always refers to a sexual urge, often a disordered one. We now know that sexual activity can represent a range of responses, from loving commitment to cruel domination; and physical intimacy can be both a sign of generous love and an indication of needy dependency. In every case, the antidote is the same: Practicing the cardinal virtues of fortitude, temperance, justice, and prudence. Fortitude allows us to stand up against the values of society that are contrary to those of the Gospel. Guided by temperance, partners learn that genuine concern for one another makes genuine pleasure possible. Justice recognizes the human dignity of every person, and refuses to exploit that dignity. Prudence regulates our actions and helps us to avoid situations that might lead to promiscuous or casual sex.

Anger is called for and appropriate in many situations. There is little in life so satisfying as a good burst of rage – sometimes called "righteous indignation." However, most of us find ourselves getting angry when our convenience or authority is being challenged. In these cases, a Christian should watch out for anger disproportionate to the offense.

Gluttony is a national problem, for consumption is embedded into our culture. The Church cautions moderation and temperance in our consumption so that we do not lose sight of our primary end – God. Eating is not just a personal need but a communal act. It puts us in touch with the mysteries of the universe as well as its harsh realities: In order to live, everything on earth must eat something else.

Sins that arise from gluttony tend to overemphasize one dimension of eating or drinking to the exclusion of others: overdoing the personal while ignoring the communal, elevating the spiritual at the expense of the natural. Moderation and temperance, balancing fasting and feasting, help to counteract this sinful human tendency.

Sloth is an old English word for "laziness." In moral theology, sloth is defined as "disgust with the spiritual because of the physical effort involved." Living the Christian life is not a thrill a minute. Sanctification is a long, hard, gradual process. Those who are "turned off" by God, by the Church, by the work for peace and justice, and so on may well be victims of sloth. For them the joy is gone. The cure is action, even painful action, because there is no gain without pain.

No matter what sinful habit has beset us, we can rejoice that we need not stay in that darkness. By God's grace, we can once again turn toward the light: through Baptism, through Reconciliation, through the other sacraments, and by hearing the Word of God. In this way we continue to walk in the light of Christ. We who were born blind, by God's grace can now truly see!

TWENTY-EIGHT

A National Examination of Conscience

*Woe to those who call evil good and good evil,
who put darkness for light and light for darkness,
who put bitter for sweet and sweet for bitter!*

Isaiah 5:20

By way of the Internet I received an article out of the St. Robert Parish bulletin, which reproduced a prayer offered by a Protestant pastor earlier that year at the opening of the state Senate of Kansas. The response to the prayer, I am told, was immediate and widespread. Though several senators walked out during the prayer in protest, within six weeks Reverend Joe Wright received more than 5000 phone calls – only 47 of whom responded negatively. I offer it to you here as a "national examination of conscience."

Heavenly Father, we come before you today to ask your forgiveness and to seek your direction and guidance. We know that your word says, 'Woe to those who call evil good,' but that is exactly what we have done. We have lost our spiritual equilibrium and reversed our values. We confess that.

We have ridiculed the absolute truth of your Word and called it Pluralism.

We have worshipped other gods and called it Multiculturalism.

We have endorsed perversion and called it Alternative Lifestyle.

We have exploited the poor and called it the Lottery.

We have rewarded laziness and called it Welfare.

We have killed our unborn and called it Choice.

We have shot abortionists and called it Justifiable.

We have neglected to discipline our children and called it Self-Esteem.

We have abused power and called it Politics.

We have coveted our neighbor's possessions and called it Ambition.

We have polluted the air with profanity and pornography and called it Freedom of Expression.

We have ridiculed the time-honored values of our forefathers and called it Enlightenment.

Search us, O God, and know our hearts today. Cleanse us from every sin and set us free. Guide and bless these men and women who have been sent to direct us to the center of your will. We ask it in the name of your Son, the living Savior, Jesus Christ. Amen.

TWENTY-NINE

You Are Salt

———••——

*"You are the salt of the earth; but if salt has lost its taste,
how shall its saltiness be restored?"*

Matthew 5:13

The New Testament contains seven strong statements by Jesus, John, Paul, and Peter that begin with "You are..." Each of these statements challenges us to live up to the basics of the Christian religion. Over the course of the next few days, we will look at each of them.

The first of these is salt. "You are the salt of the earth..." Jesus tells us. But what does this mean? The encyclopedia indicates that in modern life there are 1400 different uses for salt. It flavors food. Meat packers, chemical plants, tanneries, and refrigeration processes all use salt. Salt takes ice off roads, helps to freeze ice cream, softens water, and is used to feed livestock.

Salt was the chief economic product of ancient times. "Sel" (in Latin) was so valuable it was used the same as money. The Roman army was often paid with it – hence the word, "salary." A person "worth is salt" is someone deserving of his or her pay.

Palestinian salt wasn't always pure and sometimes underwent chemical changes (as in the Dead Sea area to this day), making it tasteless and worthless. When Jesus called His followers "the salt of the earth," He was saying that we give flavor to God's earth. We make creation pleasing to God!

Surrounded as we are by evil, we could get discouraged. The false values promoted by the media and so many celebrities, and that appeal to so many people, might make us wonder whether Christianity is relevant. Those who thumb their noses at the Commandments (and seem to get away with it) make us question the importance of virtue. (Then again, in Genesis 19 when God ordered Lot and his family to flee Sodom and Gomorrah and not look back, Lot's wife disobeyed and was turned into a pillar of salt!)

If we give up our gospel values – that is, if our salt goes flat – and we lose our Christian flavor, what is left to please our God? About thirty years ago, we used to put a pinch of salt on the tongue of each candidate for Baptism, and say: "Receive the salt of wisdom; may it be helpful to you for everlasting life." The lesson was clear to adults; infants invariably reacted to the taste of the salt, giving parents an opportunity to explain what was happening to children old enough to understand what was happening.

As we look at our lives, we need to ask ourselves: "Am I worth my salt?" May the Lord give us grace to keep us from going flat, and help us to retain our Christian flavor.

THIRTY

You Are Strangers in Exile

Beloved, you are strangers and in exile... Though the pagans
may slander you... conduct yourselves blamelessly among them.
By observing your good works, they may give glory to God.

2 Peter 2:11-12

The history of Abraham, Isaac, Jacob, Moses and the rest of the
Jewish people is one long series of wanderings and struggles in
search of a home. Jesus Himself, Creator of all, did not seem to be
at home here on earth. Born in a barn, Jesus once remarked that
birds have nests but the Son of Man had no place to lay His head.
He didn't even have a tomb of His own.

No wonder, then, that when the first Christians were being
chased, arrested, and even killed, St. Peter exhorted them to remember that they were strangers in exile. St. Paul, seeing opposition to
Christianity on all sides, told his readers, "Our home is in heaven,"
and "We have here no lasting city."

Years ago, during the Cold War, I was a stranger for four
weeks in eight European and Middle Eastern countries. I clutched
my passport everywhere I went, never for a minute forgetting my
American citizenship. Most people treated me well; it helped that I
had American Express traveler's checks. However, two or three
incidents reminded me that the foreign tourists always have a disad-
vantage. I had been warned by the State Department not to get
involved in anything political or military, so I showed scrupulous
respect for the host countries. Even so, I got sick three times when I
ate local food or drank local water. Their cultures, languages, ideas,

and standards were so different from mine that I was glad to get back home to the good ol' U.S.A.

In much the same way, you and I are strangers and exiles in this world. God's world is good, and our sojourn here is God's will. However, we are to be IN the world and not OF it. There is a real sense in which the world is our enemy and in fundamental opposition to everything Jesus stands for.

St. Paul reminds us: "your citizenship is in heaven." Baptism is our passport. And yet, if we get too caught up in the care, riches and pleasures of this life, it places our heavenly citizenship in jeopardy. The standards, values and ideas of the world, the media, and the cultural elite are not those of the Christ of the Gospel.

The Blessed Virgin Mary lived as a refugee in Egypt for the safety of her Son. Yet she was not afraid to say "Yes" to God, whatever that might mean. She knew the loneliness of the widow, and the agony of losing a son. She identified with all those who are rejected, despised, and pushed around. She gives hope to those who struggle for a more just world; she challenges us all to live a simpler life, a life of unconditional trust in the loving care of our Heavenly Father and our King.

THIRTY-ONE

You Are a Letter of Christ

Clearly you are a letter of Christ that I have delivered,
a letter written not with ink but by the Spirit of the living God,
not on tablets of stone but on tablets of flesh in the heart.

1 Corinthians 3:3

St. Francis of Assisi used to tell his followers: "Preach the Gospel always, and when necessary use words." A Holy Cross priest from Notre Dame, who volunteered some years ago to work in Chile with my missionary cousin, asked to come back to the States two years later. As hard as he had tried, his Irish tongue just could not accommodate itself to the Spanish language. The mission superior, however, pleaded that he stay because of the good influence of this young religious on the Chilean natives.

Years ago in my Minnesota diocese, priests told me of a farewell dinner for a Catholic priest who was being transferred from Grand Forks Air Base across the river in North Dakota. The chaplain embarrassed the pilot in his remarks: The pilot had been responsible for twelve airmen becoming Catholics, entirely by his example of manly Christian living.

These are instances of persons St. Paul would have called "letters of Christ." Their everyday living out the faith positively influenced those around them. St. Paul is responsible for thirteen epistles, eloquent New Testament letters that had a tremendous impact on the early Christian communities. Yet Paul modestly asserts that his writings amount to little. "You are," he says to his readers, "the letter of Christ that I have delivered."

Many years ago a report was released by the Bill Graham Evangelistic Association, which surveyed churches to find out "How Do People Come into Church Membership?" As it turns out, 6 to 8 percent just walk in off the street and ask to join. Quality programs draw another 2 to 3 percent. Pastors attract 8 to 12 percent by their eloquence, personality, or compassion. People with special needs, such as comfort in bereavement or courage to face a terminal illness, account for another 3 to 4 percent. Children in religious education or Sunday school influence 5 to 8 percent of adults entering or returning to church. However, *friends and relatives count for seventy-five to eighty percent of all conversions and returns to religious practice.*

You, dear reader, are a Letter of Christ. All sorts of people are "reading" you every day. The bigoted, the curious, the young, the weak, the hero-worshipers and the saints – all are observing you every day. In fact, you may be the only letter of Christ that some people ever see. In everyday things, in everyday ways, dozens of people are looking to you all the time. They are reading your life like a book, because "clearly you are a letter of Christ."

THIRTY-TWO

You Are Children of God

*God sent his Son, born of a woman, born under the law,
to ransom those under the law, so that we might receive
adoption. As proof that you are children, God sent the spirit
of his Son into our hearts, crying out, "Abba, Father!"*

Galatians 4:4-6

This passage from St. Paul's letter to the Galatians is drawn from the culture of his time. By emancipation and adoption, even slaves could enjoy the goods, rights, and privileges of Roman families. In his first epistle, St. John marvels at this fact of divine adoption for the baptized: "See what love the Father has bestowed on us in letting us be called children of God! Yet that is what we are" (1 John 3:1).

This New Testament teaching is not just a beautiful thought or a figure of speech or a pious flight of imagination. It is a glorious reality. It is THE amazing grace: You are a child of God! Made in God's image, you have been remade in Baptism. "Justified by the gift of God through the redemption wrought in Christ Jesus" (Romans 3:24), you meet all the conditions of real adoption. You are children of God, "heirs as well, heirs of God and joint heirs with Christ" (Romans 8:17).

Of course, being a child of God requires a certain type of behavior. The French have a term for it: *noblesse oblige* (the obligations of nobility). Queen Elizabeth and Prince Philip have four children, several of whom in recent years have given their parents grief. No doubt she has had to remind them on occasion that nobility has obligations.

You and I have a much higher status than the children of the Royal House of Windsor-Mountbatten. We are children of the Eternal King.

This truth, rightly understood, should instill in us a profound sense of gratitude. Failure to thank God for His generosity to us leads to fuzzy thinking. So what does such genuine gratitude look like?

First of all, it is *penitential.* On his first pastoral visit to the United States, in 1979, Pope John Paul II exhorted us to give not just from our surplus but from our need. "Left-over" giving may mark us as decent, civilized human beings; but there is hardly anything truly Christian, saintly or even commendable about this kind of sharing.

Our gratitude must be *confident.* Gratitude is essentially the confidence that, whatever may come our way, God will take care of us. To be grateful even in the midst of tragedy is to have the healthy conviction that God "writes straight with crooked lines," that all things really do work out for good to those who love Him.

Finally, gratitude must be *practical.* Our thanks is to be demonstrated through love. Having been made eternally rich through Christ, we are to offer gifts of gratitude for humanity's needs. Those of us who have experienced the generosity of God will one day be asked to give account, as good stewards of God's riches. Will your life be marked by gratitude – or selfishness?

THIRTY-THREE

You Are the Temple of God

———⊷◆⊶———

Are you not aware that you are the temple of God,
and that the Spirit of God dwells in you?…
The temple of God is holy, and you are that temple.

1 Corinthians 3:16-17

The Roman Empire at the time of the apostles was rotten with sexual immorality. The cult of the body held sway, and sexual acts were part of the worship in major temples. Prostitution, homosexual acts and venereal diseases were rampant, as we read in the first chapter of the Epistle to the Romans.

The tiny Christian communities sprouting up in Asia Minor, Greece and Italy were thus surrounded by perversions and desecrations that evoked this warning by the Apostle Paul to the believers in the seaport town of Corinth: "You are the temple of God." Your bodies are holy!

The warning seems just as timely to us. In the cities and towns of the U.S.A., worse things than those in Romans are commonplace. The holiness of our bodies is proclaimed loud and clear by the sacramental rites in which they are washed, anointed, fed regularly with the Bread of Heaven, incensed occasionally, tenderly prepared for death and buried in consecrated ground.

As a result of this elevation of the human being by grace, even our physical functions are holy. That is why it is said that cleanliness is next to godliness. That is why food and drink are sanctified by prayer. And that is why, for the believer, sex is more than mere physical mating. For the Christian, sex is a special gift of

God and a sharing in God's creative power.

Some forty-five years ago, in what is now the Gayloard diocese, I visited an elderly Catholic gentleman in his rural home. The old-fashioned parlor with its tall windows, antique settees and working Victorola had a small table in the center under a handsome brass chandelier. The table was covered with a white cloth.

Some years before this visit, St. Rose Church up the road had burned down one night while the pastor was away. Neighbors had saved what they could from the burning building, and the Blessed Sacrament had been brought to this gentleman's home. He and his family kept vigil until the pastor returned the next day.

The elderly gentleman told me the story in hushed tones. His parlor had been God's temple for one night. Years later he was still awed by it and had to show me this special room and the special table.

You are holy like a temple, like a tabernacle, like that parlor, like that table, because the Spirit of God dwells within you.

THIRTY-FOUR

You Are a Royal Priesthood

You, however, are a chosen race,
a royal priesthood,
a holy nation,
a people he claims for his own
to proclaim the glorious works of the One who called you...

1 Peter 2:9

Part of the Counter-Reformation heritage was an emphasis on the sacramental, ministerial priesthood. The sixteenth-century Protestant preachers were attacking it and emphasizing instead the priesthood of all believers. The natural Catholic reaction was to purge the ministerial priesthood of abuses and then to stress it energetically.

As a result, for four hundred years the doctrine of the priesthood of all believers suffered benign neglect among us. It was always acknowledged in our theology, but also accompanied by a caution: Remember there is a basic difference between the ordained priesthood and the royal priesthood of the faithful, a difference of kind and not just degree.

Today the emphasis is in the other direction – not cautionary but rather encouraging. First Peter is a "general epistle" addressed to the whole Church. There is no reference in 1 Peter 2 to the Eucharist or to the priestly ministry connected with it. All Christians constitute a royal priesthood. You, too, are priests.

This is a priesthood that, as 1 Peter 2:5 teaches, manifests itself in "offering spiritual sacrifices acceptable to God." It is a priesthood of offering sanctified lives through all that we do. This, the priesthood that we share, is the one that makes us saints. Some are called out of it into the ordained, ministerial priesthood. Even so, these men are a part of the priesthood of all believers first. It is a great, good news that "you are a royal priesthood."

The Book of Revelation praises Christ the Lamb for this. "You ransomed for God men and women from every tribe and tongue and people and nation, making them a kingdom of priests to our God" (Revelation. 5:9-10).

THIRTY-FIVE

You Are the People of God

*But you are... a consecrated nation, a people set apart to
sing the praises of God who called you out of darkness
into his own wonderful light. Once you were not a people at all,
but now you are the People of God.*

1 Peter 2:9-10

The Scriptures use many images and figures to describe the Church, none of them more complimentary than St. Peter's designation as the new "People of God." In the Old Testament, God chose the race of Israel and set up a covenant with them, calling on Israel to acknowledge Him in truth and to serve Him in holiness.

"They will be my people, and I will be their God" was the bare-bones statement of that covenant relationship, sealed in the blood of animals by Moses on Mount Sinai. All this was by way of preparation for the "new and everlasting covenant" established by Jesus and sealed with His own precious blood on Mount Calvary.

The new People of God come from many nations, not just one. Their heritage is the dignity and freedom of the children of God in whose hearts the Holy Spirit dwells as in a temple. Their law is to love one another the way Christ loved us. Their goal is the kingdom of God, already begun here on earth and awaiting fulfillment at the end of time. As we read in *Lumen Gentium* (33):

> *Gathered together in the People of God and established in
> the one Body of Christ under one head, the laity – no matter
> who they are – have, as living members, the vocation of*

applying to the building up of the Church....

The apostolate of the laity is a sharing in the salvific message of the Church.... [Making] the Church present and fruitful in those places and circumstances where it is only through them that she can become the salt of the earth.

We are a people of light. Darkness covered the whole land on the Friday afternoon when Christ died, and dark was the tomb where His lifeless body lay Friday night and Saturday. In darkness you assemble Saturday night for the watch of the Resurrection. Christ your light calls you then out of darkness, radiant in His Easter glory. Of all the seven titles we have discussed — salt, strangers, letters, temples, children, royal priesthood – by far the noblest of them all is this last one. You are a People of God!

Section Five

Questions People Ask Me

THIRTY-SIX

What Makes the Church "Catholic"?

Then the righteous will answer, "Lord, when did we see thee
hungry and feed thee, or thirsty and give thee drink? And when
did we see thee a stranger and welcome thee...?" And the
King will answer them, "Truly, I say to you, as you did it to
one of the least of these my brethren, you did it to me."

Matthew 25:37-40

As the grandson of immigrants from eastern Europe, and as the son of first-generation parents, I know something about ethnic parishes. And as a churchman who helped to organize and develop ethnic parishes for Hispanics and Asiatics in Michigan, I say that they were and still are necessary. The flowering of the Catholic Church in the United States into a real *koinonia* (Greek) or *communio* (Latin) – that is, a fellowship, partnership, or mutual sharing – has been made possible by the success of the ethnic parish.

For the Vietnamese on Lansing's south side, St. Andrew Dung-Lac Parish is the most recent example of this. Beginning in 1980, with the influx of Vietnamese refugees into the Lansing area, the diocese obtained the services of Father Joseph Tran, himself a refugee, to minister to them in the cathedral. I began attending religious and cultural events in this community. For fourteen years, for example, I celebrated Mass for them early on Christmas Eve with Father Tran interpreting the homily. Afterwards I had a Vietnamese dinner with the community and enjoyed an after-dinner program, interpreted to me by bilingual grade-schoolers.

My memories of early 1980s were that the elders of the community, the grandparents, always looked sad. They missed their homeland, didn't understand or speak English, and seemed lost. They were reverent, polite, and appreciative of American freedom; but their hearts were in the past. Their sons and daughters had the same struggles; but, working very hard, they fared much better.

Among the Vietnamese today, it is the grandchildren of the first refugees who are the first to be really at home in American society, both civic and religious. It was the same with my family years ago. Of the eleven children born to my immigrant grandparents, only the two youngest daughters married outside the ethnic circle. But of the twenty-four cousins whom my parents, aunts, and uncles begot, nineteen married non-Poles, only one of whom was non-Catholic.

The ethnic parishes kept the faith alive for European immigrants and their children. The grandchildren of these immigrants were the ones who intermarried, made the European ethnic parishes extinct, and brought about the diversity that makes the Church truly *catholic* – that is, truly universal in scope. When we welcome these newcomers among us, we welcome the Lord Himself, who commended His faithful followers: "I was a stranger, and you took me in" (Matthew 25:43).

THIRTY-SEVEN

What's So Important About the Sabbath?

———➤◆◄———

*Rightly, then, the Psalmist's cry is applied to Sunday:
"This is the day which the Lord has made: let us rejoice and
be glad in it" (Ps 118:24). This invitation to joy, which the
Easter liturgy makes its own, reflects the astonishment which
came over the women who, having seen the crucifixion of Christ,
found the tomb empty when they went there "very early on the
first day after the Sabbath" (Mk 16:2). It is an invitation to
relive in some way the experience of the two disciples of Emmaus,
who felt their hearts "burn within them" as the Risen One
walked with them on the road, explaining the Scriptures
and revealing himself in "the breaking of the bread"
(cf. Lk 24:32,35). And it echoes the joy — at first uncertain
and then overwhelming — which the Apostles experienced on
the evening of that same day, when they were visited by the
Risen Jesus and received the gift of his peace and of his Spirit
(cf. Jn 20:19-23).*

Pope John Paul II, *Dies Domini,* May 31, 1998

In his apostolic letter entitled "The Lord's Day," the Holy Father wrote in his own hand, in his native Polish, a personal letter to each of us. The letter reflects his experiences as Bishop of Krakow and his twenty years as the Bishop of Rome, and is divided into five sections: "The Day of the Lord," "The Day of Christ," "The Day of the Church," "The Day of Man(kind)," and "The Day of Days." Let us take a moment to consider each of these Sabbath names.

The Day of the Lord. The Book of Genesis describes in poetic style how God "worked" for six days to create the universe. On the seventh day, "God finished the work which he had done, and he rested... God blessed the seventh day and made it holy" (Gen 2:2-3).

This was good news indeed for the Israelites, who had endured 400 years of slavery in Egypt. At the same time, this day of joyful rest is not just for inactivity. We are to "Remember..." in order to preserve the sanctity of the Sabbath day. We owe supreme praise and thanksgiving to the One we call our Creator, God and Father.

The Day of Christ. Pope Innocent I (who led the Church from 401-414) wrote: "We celebrate Sunday because of the venerable Resurrection of our Lord Jesus Christ, and we do so not only at Easter but also at each turning of the week." The observance of Sunday rather than Saturday became one of the great distinctions between Christianity and Judaism. If the original Sabbath celebrated God's creative work, the Day of Christ celebrates our "new creation" by Baptism.

The Church's Day. Sunday is in a profound way the Church's Day. We are bound to honor God not only in private as individuals but also publicly in the Sunday assembly, where we show our solidarity with fellow believers and give witness to the world.

In his pastoral letter, the Holy Father recalls that in the first centuries of the faith, there was no need of prescribing the observance of a Sunday Eucharist. Only later, "faced with the half-heartedness or negligence of some," was the duty of attending Mass enacted into Church law. Today, the pope exhorts bishops to "ensure that Sunday is appreciated by all the faithful... to renew the remembrance of the Easter mystery in hearing the word of God and offering sacrifices to the Lord."

The Day of Man(kind). We read in Mark's Gospel, "The Sabbath was made for man, not man for the Sabbath" (Mark 2:27). It is to be a celebration for all people: a day of joy, a day of rest, and a day of mercy. This name for the Sabbath reminds us of the change in focus that takes place on this day: from preoccupation with constructive activity to a rediscovery of God's provision for us; from non-stop work to relaxation that is such a necessary part of the human experience; from self-absorption to a renewed commitment to acts of creative Christian charity. In this way, we bring into people's lives the love of Christ we have received at the Eucharistic table.

The Day of Days. The pope observes that the Christian Sunday, "like a directional arrow, cuts through human time, the months, years and centuries" and points to their target, Christ's second coming. "Sunday foreshadows the last day, the Day of the Second Coming, which in a way is already anticipated by Christ's glory in the event of the Resurrection."

In conclusion, Pope John Paul II closes his letter with these words: "The Risen Lord... calls the faithful together to give them the light of his Word and the nourishment of his Body as the perennial sacramental wellspring of redemption. The grace flowing from this wellspring renews mankind, life and history. The Spirit and the Bride say, 'Come!'" (Revelation 22:17).

THIRTY-EIGHT

Is the Mass A Repeated Sacrifice?

He took from among creation that which is bread, and gave thanks,
saying, "This is my body." The cup likewise, which is from among
the creation to which we belong, he confessed to be his blood.
He taught the new sacrifice of the new covenant, of which Malachi,
one of the twelve [minor] prophets, had signified beforehand:
"You do not do my will, says the Lord Almighty, and I will not
accept a sacrifice at your hands. For from the rising of the sun
to its setting my name is glorified among the Gentiles, and in
every place incense is offered to my name, and a pure sacrifice;
for great is my name among the Gentiles, says the Lord Almighty"
[Mal. 1:10–11]. By these words he makes it plain that the former
people will cease to make offerings to God; but that in every place
sacrifice will be offered to him, and indeed, a pure one, for
his name is glorified among the Gentiles.

St. Irenaeus, Against Heresies 4:17:5 [A.D. 189]

For generations I taught catechism classes that there are four movements in the Mass: We speak to God, God speaks to us (the Mass of the Catechumens); we give our gifts to God, God gives His Gift to us (the Mass of the Faithful). The giving parts are the Holy Sacrifice. Every Christmas, I hear from people, now grandparents, who still remember those phrases.

From the beginning of the Church, Christians have celebrated the Eucharist in substantially the same way, bound as we are by the command of the Lord, "Do this in remembrance of me." On Holy Thursday night He said, "This is my body, which is given for you…. This cup, which is poured out for you, is the New Covenant in my blood." On Good Friday He gave His body for us and poured out His blood for us on the cross. In the Eucharist Christ gives us the very body He gave up for us on the cross, the very blood that He "poured out for many for the forgiveness of sins."

Protestants deny that the Eucharist is a sacrifice, and accuse us of believing that we crucify Christ over and over again every day. The truth is that we Catholics (as well as the Eastern Orthodox) believe the Eucharist makes present the sacrifice of the Cross and is *one single sacrifice* with the sacrifice on Calvary. The Eucharist is the bloodless sacrifice of the cross, but the victim is one and the same. Only the manner is different. In the bloody manner, Christ offered Himself once for all (Hebrews 7:27).

This recurring offering was commanded by Lord Himself, who told the apostles at the Last Supper to repeat His actions and His words "in remembrance of me." St. Paul is clear on our purpose in doing this: "For as often as you eat this bread and drink the cup, you proclaim the death of the Lord until he comes" (1 Corinthians 11:26).

This is why, as the Eucharistic liturgy developed, every celebration included the remembering of what Jesus did for us. In a prayer called by the Greek term *anamnesis,* we REMEMBER the passion, death and resurrection of the Lord immediately after the words of consecration of the bread and wine.

In the two Eucharistic prayers you probably hear most often in your parish, the celebrant says: "In memory of His death and resurrection, we offer you, Father, this life-giving bread, this saving cup" or "Father, calling to mind the death your Son endured for our salvation, His glorious resurrection and ascension into heaven, and ready to greet Him when he comes again, we offer you in thanksgiving this holy and living sacrifice."

The very words of institution show that the Eucharist has a sacrificial as well as a memorial character. "This is my body which will be given for you… This is my blood which will be shed for you." Hence in the anamnesis we say "life-giving bread," "saving cup," "holy and living sacrifice." In memory of Him, mystically and sacramentally, the Eucharist makes present again in an unbloody way the sacrifice of Christ.

THIRTY-NINE

Why Go to Confession?

———————

Therefore confess your sins to one another, and pray for
one another, that you may be healed. The prayer of a
righteous man has great power in its effects.

James 5:16

If you ask me to share with you the most powerful and most beautiful experiences I have had in the ministry of reconciliation, I
have to say they were the mammoth celebrations we had in each of
the then five regions of the diocese during Lent in 1979 and 1980.

Held in the biggest gymnasiums we could find, with the
bishop presiding on Sunday afternoons and general absolution
offered (with the stipulation that really grave sins should be
included in the next private confession), thousands of penitents
attended.

An exhortation to repentance and an assurance of God's
readiness to forgive all sincere comers was followed by an adult
examination of conscience. This was a key factor, I was told later
by many people who had been reciting the formulas and the lists of
sins the sisters taught them in grade school. In all five regions,
adults who had been away from the sacraments since the end of the
Second Vatican Council thanked me in tears in the halls and in the
parking lots.

I still keep a letter sent to me by an eighty-six-year-old lady,
a pious Catholic who said she spoke for many relatives and friends
her own age. The adult liturgy of the afternoon, which took an hour,
had taught them much, she insisted. "What a joy, what peace of

mind for us older people, some of us scrupulous, doubtful, fearful, with failing memories, and in need of assurance as we get ready to leave this world."

Pastors in all five regions reported after the regional penance services that there was a notable increase in the number of persons coming to the rectory seeking to have marriages regularized, or inquiring about annulment procedures, or seeking advice on making restitution for actions in the past. The people who flocked to these penance services were not renegades or strangers, mafia types or bigamists, looking for cheap grace. They were regular members of parishes and regular church-goers who had grown lax in the confusing years following the Second Vatican Council.

Six months after the last of these events, a letter from the papal nuncio in Washington ordered all bishops to stop conducting such services or allowing them in their dioceses. Pope Paul VI had given something special to the Church... Now the Sacrament of Penance and Reconciliation has fallen upon hard times. New initiatives are needed in the Church to restore reconciliation as a part of Catholic spiritual life again.

For some time now, there have been signs that some Protestant groups – including both Evangelicals and Pentecostals – are recognizing the spiritual value of penitence. In the Easter 1993 issue of *The Christian Century,* a Protestant ecumenical weekly, was an article about the comeback of the ancient penitential tradition in Protestant circles. Noting that more and more Protestants are lining up on Ash Wednesday to get ashes on their foreheads, the article suggests that the next step is to move from word and symbol (liturgy) to concrete action (penance).

Two theologians are cited as advocates of taking seriously the ancient Christian practice of penance. Horace T. Allen, professor at Boston University (Baptist) School of Theology, emphasizes the social dimensions of sin and the idea of reconciliation that our sacramental theology has stressed since Vatican II. Stephen Long, a United Methodist professor at Duke Divinity School, wrote in a newsletter published at Duke, "Without penance, forgiveness is cheap; and cheap forgiveness is a sign that we have not taken sin seriously."

May the Spirit continue to move among us and bring a fresh attitude of penance and reconciliation among us, that we may be more truly and completely unified as the one true Body of Christ.

FORTY

Where Is Heaven?

Eye has not seen, ear has not heard, nor has it so much as dawned on man what God has prepared for those who love him.

1 Corinthians 2:9

Twice a year, the week before Christmas and the week before Easter, the cover story of *Time* magazine is about some aspect of religion.... In 1997, *Time* devoted its issue released during Holy Week to the question, "Does Heaven Exist?"

The question was posed, the writer said, because people seem to have foggier notions about heaven than they used to have, and they hear less about heaven from the pulpit than they formerly did. And what they hear less about now is speculation "on the architecture or the geography" of heaven – the pearly gates, the golden streets, the harps and halos, the glassy sea – mostly from the figurative verse of the book of Revelation.

The Time article sent me straight to the Catechism, to thoughtfully read all the cross-references having to do with heaven. Starting with the Creed that professes God to be "Maker of heaven and earth, of all that is, seen and unseen," and ending with the promise that our loved ones departed "are like God forever, for they 'see him as he is, face to face.'"

That is the essence of heaven. It is the eternal home of the One who loves us most.

One of Jesus' principle teachings was the Parable of the Wedding Feast (Matthew 22:1-14): "The kingdom of heaven may be likened to a king who gave a wedding feast for his son." Even today, we are drawn by the imagery to ponder the mysteries of heaven, if only on our own limited terms. The King of Heaven, who sent His Son to invite us, is waiting for us all to join the feast.

In ancient Israel, daily life was usually hard. Wedding feasts were a welcome relief from the drudgery. It should not surprise us then that our Lord compared the kingdom of heaven to what His hearers regarded as a great good. In the book of Revelation (19:9), the angel told St. John to write: "Blessed are those who have been called to the wedding feast of the Lamb." The Lamb, of course, is Jesus, the Lamb of God.

In the Eucharist, we anticipate the wedding feast of the Lamb in the heavenly Jerusalem (CCC 1329). When we receive His Body and Blood in a worthy manner, we affirm our trust in the One who claimed to be "The way, the truth, and the life" (John 14:5). Christ, the offerer and the offering, works for us to make our Eucharistic liturgy a perfect act of worship. "Through Him, with Him, in Him," all glory is given to the Divine Trinity, now and forever.

Jesus is the way. That is why we are taught to pray "through Christ our Lord." Whatever we tell the Father He will heed, whatever we ask the Father He will give, if we pray in Jesus' name. As St. Paul wrote, whatever we do, we should do in the name of Jesus as an offering to Him. Jesus is the way to give value to your prayers, works and sufferings, to your thoughts, words and actions of each day.

A prayer of Blessed Elizabeth of the Trinity gives us a beautiful vision of the joy that is to come for those who live in this reality (CCC 320):

> *O my God, Trinity whom I adore, help me forget myself entirely so to establish myself in you, unmovable and peaceful as if my soul were already in eternity. May nothing be able to trouble my peace or make me leave you, O my unchanging God, but may each minute bring me more deeply into your mystery! Grant my soul peace. Make it your heaven, your beloved dwelling and the place of your rest. May I never abandon you there, but may I be there,*

whole and entire, completely vigilant in my faith, entirely adoring, and wholly given over to your creative action.

Printed in the United States
15831LVS00004B/232-255